Types of
Thinking

'An ideal text for an introductory course on human problem-solving, reasoning and decision-making ... I'm sure this book will be popular with students and find a useful niche in many cognitive psychology courses.'

Thom Baguley, *Loughborough University*

Types of Thinking provides a basic grounding in the psychology of thinking for undergraduate students with little previous knowledge of cognitive psychology. This clear, well-structured overview explores the practical aspects and applications of everyday thinking, creative thinking, logical and scientific thinking, intelligent thinking and machine thinking. It also explores 'failures of thinking', the biases and shortcuts that sometimes lead our thinking astray. Influences on decision-making such as motivation, arousal and emotion are examined, as well as the differences between 'deep' and 'surface' thought, 'lateral' thinking, the effect of negative transfer.

The author tackles big ideas in an accessible manner and in an entertaining style, ensuring that *Types of Thinking* will be attractive not only to students but also to teachers organising and planning courses, as well as to the lay reader.

S. Ian Robertson is a Senior Lecturer in Psychology at the University of Luton.

Psychology Focus

Series editor: Perry Hinton, University of Luton

The Psychology Focus series provides students with a new focus on key topic areas in psychology. It supports students taking modules in psychology, whether for a psychology degree or a combined programme, and those renewing their qualification in a related discipline. Each short book:

■ presents clear, in-depth coverage of a discrete area with many applied examples
■ assumes no prior knowledge of psychology
■ has been written by an experienced teacher
■ has chapter summaries, annotated further reading and a glossary of key terms.

Also available in this series:

Being Ill (forthcoming)
Marian Pitts

Friendship in Childhood and Adolescence
Phil Erwin

Gender and Social Psychology
Vivien Burr

Intelligence and Abilities
Colin Cooper

Jobs, Technology and People
Nik Chmiel

Learning and Studying
James Hartley

Personality: A Cognitive Approach
Jo Brunas-Wagstaff

Psychobiology of Human Motivation
Hugh Wagner

Stereotypes, Social Cognition and Culture (forthcoming)
Perry Hinton

Stress, Cognition and Health
Tony Cassidy

Types of Thinking

- S. Ian Robertson

ROUTLEDGE

LONDON AND NEW YORK

First published 1999
by Routledge
11 New Fetter Lane
London EC4P 4EE

Simultaneously published in
the USA and Canada
by Routledge
29 West 35th Street, New York
NY 10001

Typeset in Sabon and Futura by
The Florence Group, Stoodleigh,
Devon

Printed and bound in Great Britain by
TJ International Ltd, Padstow,
Cornwall

*British Library Cataloguing in
Publication Data*
A catalogue record for this book is
available from the British Library

*Library of Congress Cataloging in
Publication Data*
Robertson, S. Ian
    Types of thinking /
        S. Ian Robertson.
        p. cm. – (Psychology focus)
    Includes bibliographical references
and index.
1. Thought and thinking.
2. Cognition.   3. Human information
processing.   I. Title.   II. Series.
BF441.R59   1999
153.4′2–dc21   98–48941
    CIP

ISBN 0–415–19105–X (hbk)

ISBN 0–415–19106–8 (pbk)

For Kathryn, Poppy and my parents

Contents

7 Thinking about thinking   133

Figures

Tables

Series preface

The Psychology Focus series provides short, up-to-date accounts of key areas in psychology without assuming the reader's prior knowledge in the subject. Psychology is often a favoured subject area for study, since it is relevant to a wide range of disciplines such as Sociology, Education, Nursing and Business Studies. These relatively inexpensive but focused short texts combine sufficient detail for psychology specialists with sufficient clarity for non-specialists.

The series authors are academics experienced in undergraduate teaching as well as research. Each takes a key topic within their area of psychological expertise and presents a short review, highlighting important themes and including both theory and research findings. Each aspect of the topic is clearly explained with supporting glossaries to elucidate technical terms.

The series has been conceived within the context of the increasing modularisation which has been developed in higher education over the last decade

and fulfils the consequent need for clear, focused, topic-based course material. Instead of following one course of study, students on a modularisation programme are often able to choose modules from a wide range of disciplines to complement the modules they are required to study for a specific degree. It can no longer be assumed that students studying a particular module will necessarily have the same background knowledge (or lack of it!) in that subject. But they will need to familiarise themselves with a particular topic rapidly since a single module in a single topic may be only 15 weeks long, with assessments arising during that period. They may have to combine eight or more modules in a single year to obtain a degree at the end of their programme of study.

One possible problem with studying a range of separate modules is that the relevance of a particular topic or the relationship between topics may not always be apparent. In the Psychology Focus series authors have drawn where possible on practical and applied examples to support the points being made so that readers can see the wider relevance of the topic under study. Also, the study of psychology is usually broken up into separate areas, such as social psychology, developmental psychology and cognitive psychology, to take three examples. Whilst the books in the Psychology Focus series will provide excellent coverage of certain key topics within these 'traditional' areas, the authors have not been constrained in their examples and explanations and may draw on material across the whole field of psychology to help explain the topic under study more fully.

Each text in the series provides the reader with a range of important material on a specific topic. They are suitably comprehensive and give a clear account of the important issues involved. The authors analyse and interpret the material as well as present an up-to-date and detailed review of key work. Recent references are provided along with suggested further reading to allow readers to investigate the topic in more depth. It is hoped, therefore, that after following the informative review of a key topic in a Psychology Focus text, readers will not only have a clear understanding of the issues in question but will be intrigued and challenged to investigate the topic further.

Chapter 1

What does 'thinking' mean?

Men fear thought as they fear nothing else on earth – more than ruin, more even than death.

Bertrand Russell,
Education: Selected Papers

There is no expedient to which a man will not resort to avoid the real labour of thinking.

Thomas A. Edison

What is thinking?

THINKING, LIKE ITS RELATED CONCEPTS 'intelligence' and 'consciousness', is something we are all intimately familiar with; and, just like intelligence and consciousness, it can be hard to define. The two quotations with which this chapter begins emphasise the effortful nature of some of our thinking and the fact that we don't particularly like to put in such effort if we can help it; nevertheless, if our lives depended on it I'm sure we could, despite what Bertrand Russell says – and, in any case, we avoid the 'real labour of thinking' because it is often a perfectly sensible thing to do. If you come face to face with a large animal with stripes and large teeth and claws, you might deduce that it is a predator. From its size you deduce that it probably preys on animals larger than you. You therefore infer that you belong to the category of prey. Since it is watching you, you deduce that it might be thinking the same thing. In such situations standing thinking is probably the last thing you want to do. Just as the shortest distance between two points is a straight line, so the quickest way to solve a problem or make a decision is often to rely on pre-packaged procedures or mental short cuts wherever possible that allow us to get things done relatively effortlessly. If you are faced with a predator a simple general rule that says 'if you see an animal bigger than you with sharp teeth, then run', is more likely to keep you alive than effortful thinking.

Doing logic puzzles, solving geometry problems, translating passages of English into French, finding ways of bringing peace to trouble-torn parts of the world, trying to remove a rusted bolt from an awkward place under a car, all involve a degree of effortful thinking. Some problems are effortful because they are not naturally occurring. The environmental pressures that existed on the grasslands of Africa hundreds of thousands of years ago were not ones that selected for our ability to write books, or work in the accountants departments of offices, or drive trucks, or do paper and pencil tests in thermodynamics. They did evolve to allow us to make plans and inferences when hunting and foraging, to understand and take part in complex social inter-action, to recognise objects, faces and dangerous situations, to identify anyone who isn't from our tribe, and so on.

Different problems require different types of thinking. In general, we don't deal with unfamiliar problems in the same way we deal with familiar ones. Not only that but people vary in the ways they prefer to think about things. Some like doing cross-word puzzles while others like making the crossword puzzles up. Some like problems where there is a definite answer whereas others like problems where there is no one right answer. Some like diagnosing what is wrong with a computer when it crashes, others like designing buildings.

We face a variety of problems daily and deal with them in a variety of ways. The aim of this book is to categorise the types of thinking we use to cope with familiar and unfamiliar situations. Much of the time it deals with the techniques we use to avoid the real labour of thinking. It also deals with the reasons why we avoid effortful thinking where we can (some of the most important ones are introduced in this chapter).

Throughout this book a number of concepts keep cropping up that are important to an understanding of thinking and its limitations. A distinction we can begin to make is between the kind of everyday thinking and problem solving that we engage in and the free-floating undirected thinking involved in dreaming.

Freud (1954) referred to two types of thinking: **primary process thinking** and **secondary process thinking**. Primary process thinking is the type governed by our instinctual drives (the id). It manifests itself mainly in dreams and daydreams where our deep rooted wishes are fulfilled. Secondary process thinking is the everyday problem solving we engage in. This too acts to fulfil our innate desires for food, sex, security, and so on, but operates within the **constraints** of the real world – which means that we can't always get what we want when we want it. You can't indulge your craving for a bar of chocolate when you are half way up a mountain and haven't brought any chocolate with you, nor is it acceptable to steal it. This book deals with the second of these two general types of thinking – the goal directed, everyday kind (for more on this distinction and on undirected thinking in particular see Gilhooly, 1996). Thinking involves a goal that has to be obtained, whether this be a dinner, a completed crossword puzzle, a medical diagnosis, or balancing a national budget. Effortful thinking is necessary when this goal is not immediately attainable and its solution is not obvious. Thinking is usually effortless when you know what to do to attain your goal.

The world in our heads

Spend a few moments thinking about what you would do if you came out of work one evening and found that your car was no longer where you left it. You may have imagined several courses of action and their possible outcomes. Your understanding of the situation and your response to it, though, are inside your head. The reason why we can make plans and predictions, achieve complex goals, and solve problems is because we can carry out a sequence of actions *in our heads* before carrying out any actions in the real world. To do that we must have a representation of the world that we can manipulate in our minds.

If I say to myself, 'There are some pretty dark clouds over there and I have to walk to the station. I'd better take an umbrella.' I am using current information (dark clouds) and relating it to current intentions and past knowledge and experience stored in long-term memory (I have to walk to the station; dark clouds often mean rain; rain makes me wet; carrying an umbrella prevents me from getting wet). Thinking therefore involves manipulating **mental representations** of the world and prevents us from making mistakes. This is an extremely useful ability.

Creating and manipulating a mental representation involves manipulating or processing information. Reading the word BREAD involves picking out the lines and curves of the letters, sticking them together to form letters, recognising letters, recognising the word, converting the written letters or groups of letters into sounds, accessing the word's pronunciation. Each stage involves some kind of processing of the information produced at the earlier stage to build up to the final pronunciation. These stages don't necessarily occur one after the other. They could be operating in parallel at almost the same time (see Chapter 6). The simplest activity such as reading this sentence out loud requires a vast amount of extremely fast, automatic processes that are not under conscious control. You can't stop yourself from understanding the word BREAD. You recognise it as a real word; know what it sounds like; you know what it means; you know it is commonly associated with the word BUTTER. At its most basic level, then, thinking is information processing.

The limits to thinking

An operation such as multiplying 2×3 in your head does not involve much processing. In fact you probably retrieve the answer as a fact straight from long-term memory. Multiplying 378 by 463 in your head is different. You probably don't have the answer stored in long-term memory for a start, so it becomes the kind of problem you have to think about. You need to access relevant bits of information from memory, including the relevant method for doing this kind of problem, and break the problem down into manageable sub-problems. You need to access the results of multiplying 8 by 3 and what to do with the 2 and 4 and so on. It is

5

hard to keep all the information from earlier stages of problem solving in your mind without writing it down. The mental workspace that does the multiplying, temporarily stores the answers you get, and accesses the relevant bits of information from long-term memory, is known as **working memory** (Baddeley, 1986, 1997). Solving problems therefore involves storage and rehearsal of information as well as processing bits of information in working memory, which is in turn made more or less difficult (uses up more or less processing capacity) depending on the knowledge of the solver (Just, Carpenter and Hemphill, 1996; Kyllonen and Christal, 1990). Our thinking is limited because the capacity to store and process information is limited. The short-term store has a capacity of about seven bits or 'chunks' of information (Miller, 1956) although Simon (1974) puts it at around five chunks, but this gets smaller the more work we have to do to that information. Thinking gets more effortful as we push working memory to its limits and errors can occur when it is overloaded.

Rational thinking

We would like to think of ourselves as rational beings. When we look around at what we do to each other and the environment, or at arguments between groups of people to which we do not belong, our thinking does not look all that rational. Part of the confusion is that 'rational' has two meanings. The first is synonymous with logical thinking. Rational thinking is what you do when you are thinking logically. The second meaning refers to the extent to which our thinking is related to our goals. Whenever we try to get what we want in the easiest possible way we know how, then we are acting rationally. To be more precise: if we weren't limited in our capacity to store and process information temporarily, if we could access all the relevant information from our long-term memory when we needed it, if we were aware of our prior beliefs and attitudes and their effect on our thinking, if we were aware of our own best interests, and if we could do all that in pursuit of our goals then we would be thinking rationally. Unfortunately, as you may have learned from bitter experience, our ability to do those things is limited. As a result our **rationality** is **bounded** (Simon, 1983). It has its limits. Those limits have already been discussed as they are the limits in our capacity to process information and retrieve it when we need it.

As a result of processing limits we don't have the capacity and don't have the time to identify and process all the information relevant to a problem. If we are looking for a decent restaurant that's not too dear, we don't tend to go around comparing all the menus and all the prices of all the restaurants in a two-mile radius. Instead, we have certain criteria and the first restaurant we come to that meets those criteria is likely to be the one we choose. This is known as **satisficing** (Simon, 1956), a blend of *satisfying* and *sufficing*. The first restaurant, solution, man, woman, bus that comes along that satisfies some basic minimum criteria suffices.

Surface thinking and deep thinking

> The human understanding is most excited by that which strikes and enters the mind at once and suddenly, and by which the imagination is immediately filled and inflated. It then begins almost imperceptibly to conceive and suppose that everything is similar to the few objects which have taken possession of the mind.
>
> (Francis Bacon, *Novum Organum*)

Several centuries ago Francis Bacon realised that there were two important influences on our thinking: salience and similarity. We have evolved to take particular note of the salient features of our environment; we notice whatever stands out. In trying to understand an unfamiliar situation or problem we latch onto the aspects that seem to stand out. Unfortunately, what appears to be salient may not in fact be relevant and one's thinking can be 'led up the garden path'. This simple but wide-reaching fact can account for the errors students make when learning new topics, why advertisements are written the way they are, why the media exert a powerful influence over how we think, why we can be prejudiced. Here are some examples:

1 Physics students were asked to categorise cards containing examples of physics problems according to their similarity. Undergraduate students categorised them according to the **'surface features'** of the problems (keywords, pulleys, ramps, weights, and so on). Ph.D. students categorised them according to the **'structural features'**: the underlying principles of Newtonian mechanics involved (Chi, Feltovich and Glaser, 1981).

2 If an advert in a clothes shop says 'Up to £5 off' people might be led to believe they are likely to get £5 off what they buy since the £5 'stands out' (although one garment in the whole shop might have £5 off and the rest 50p).

3 On hearing a report of a man who had to have several major operations because he started eating bran-based breakfast cereal people may give up eating such cereals. Memorable cases stick in the mind – they stand out – and influence subsequent thinking. The alternatives (the millions of people who eat breakfast cereals containing bran and are perfectly healthy) are ignored.

4 Prejudice avoids the need for thinking. A feature of a person that stands out (colour or gender) is used as the basis for making judgements about that person (is aggressive, can't cook) without the need for evidence.

Because of the limits of our capacity to process information, our rationality – our ability to choose the best path to achieve our goals – is also limited. When faced with an unfamiliar situation we have, therefore, to rely on those aspects of the situation that stand out in some way. The representation we form of a problem is often based on salient surface features. To go beyond this kind of surface thinking we need to be aware of the structural features of a task or situation, or, when the problem is an unfamiliar one, to make an effort to explore the problem in some depth. This is 'deep' thinking. Chapter 2 looks at these aspects of problem solving in more detail and examines the processes involved in both everyday thinking (usually about familiar problems) and in dealing with unfamiliar problems. It also looks at what happens when we have the wrong mental representation of everyday physics.

Chapter 3 discusses creative thinking. Once again the kind of representation one has of a situation is important. Often breaking free of a faulty or incomplete representation can lead to a creative insight. Such insights are often the result of deep thinking since they require an understanding of a problem's underlying structure. Creative solutions to problems can also come about by discovering a useful analogy, and analogies can also help people understand new concepts.

Chapter 4 explores the idea that children's thinking is different in kind from that of adults and examines the development of thinking from early childhood to 'formal' thinking in adulthood. It then goes on to look at logical thinking and why we seem to be good at some kinds of reasoning and poor at others.

Chapter 5 focuses on the various ways in which relying on surface thinking lets us down. The short cuts we use in everyday thinking sometimes let us down. Furthermore, we have biases in our thinking that cause us to focus more on some aspects of problems and ignore others. Beliefs, attitudes, prejudices, emotions all tend to muddy the waters of thought.

Chapter 6 concentrates on intelligent thinking and what that means. Various models of intelligence are discussed and the chapter goes on to look at whether machines can think and can be said to have intelligence.

Chapter 7 presents a summary of the ideas in the previous chapters and looks at the ramifications of the limits to our capacity to process information and at our bias towards attending to those aspects of the environment that stand out.

Summary

Thinking is influenced by the kinds of mental representations we form of a situation which can make thinking either effortful or effortless. Everyday thinking tends to be effortless since it usually involves problems we are familiar with. Unfamiliar problems often require more effort.

Thinking involves processing information. Some forms of thinking are effortful because they make great demands on our limited capacity processing system. As a result we tend to adopt strategies such as satisficing or relying on surface features of a situation to guide our thinking to get over these limitations.

Chapter 2

Everyday thinking

11

Civilisation advances by extending the number of important operations which we can perform without thinking.

(Alfred North Whitehead, *Adventures of Ideas*)

The only reason some people get lost in thought is because it's unfamiliar territory.

(Attributed to Paul Fix)

THIS CHAPTER CONCENTRATES ON two types of everyday thinking: the 'mundane' or routine thinking that gets us by every day and that involves little effort – such as making routine plans, decisions and judgements, categorising, and so on; and the kinds of thinking and problem solving that require some degree of effort – such as deciding what to prepare for dinner, doing puzzles, diagnosing illnesses, and writing essays. Understanding thinking requires an understanding of how we deal with the information available to us from the environment and from the knowledge we already have. More specifically the chapter looks at how thinking and problem solving can be understood in terms of sub-goaling (Anderson, 1993; Newell and Simon, 1972), where a problem is broken down into manageable chunks. Breaking a problem down into smaller 'sub-problems' makes finding a solution easier and is one of several methods we use when we engage in a 'mental search' for a solution.

It was pointed out in Chapter 1 that our ability to think through complex or unfamiliar problems is limited by the capacity limitations of our information processing system. Our 'mental workspace' is limited both in how much information it can hold and in how much work it can do on that information. We are not always able to access relevant information from memory when it is needed. We may not notice what features of the environment are relevant to our current needs. We often focus on immediately apparent surface characteristics of situations (the way an advert is worded, the rhetoric of an argument, etc.) which influence how we think of those situations. In short, our 'rationality' is limited.

However, we do develop fairly powerful strategies for getting round these limitations by relying on those features of the environment that seem to be predictive. Everyday thinking often relies on the context in which the thinking takes place. The environment around us, including the problem environment, presents us with information that we may or may not make use of when we think. For example, people who use computers a lot rely on pull-down menus but would be often unable to say exactly what was under each menu. Instead they tend to rely on the environment (menus, icons, etc.) to help them find what they want without having to memorise where everything is. Thus, problems can be characterised in terms of the amount of information they contain that might help solve them.

Apart from using the environment, another way of making sense of the world is to develop working hypotheses about all kinds of things: from how someone will cope under stress, to how evaporation works, to how a device works. These working hypotheses can take the form of a kind of model in our heads of how systems work, which we use to make predictions and guide our actions. This chapter and the next therefore stress the importance of mental representations since the type of representation we form of a situation will determine the kinds of thinking we engage in.

Life's little problems

Imagine that after a tiring day you want to sit in a comfortable chair with a glass of beer and watch television. As you are about to sit on the sofa you notice that it is covered in cat hairs, so you go into the kitchen and look in the cupboard under the sink for a brush to clean it. The brush doesn't seem to be there. Eventually you find it in an adjacent cupboard and take it to the living room to clean the sofa. You now have a small pile of cat hairs to get rid of so you take it and the brush back into the kitchen and put the brush back where it belongs and the cat hairs in the bin. You wash your hands and head back to the living room and then realise that you haven't yet got your glass of beer. You fetch the beer from the fridge and a glass from the cupboard where the glasses are kept. You open the can and pour your drink. You go back to the living room and sit down. The next thing you realise you don't have the remote control for the TV. You look to either side of you. You can't see it. You have to stand up again and begin a more widespread search. There it is between the cushions on the sofa. You point it at the TV and press the button. Nothing happens. You try again. And again. The TV remains silent. Maybe there's something wrong with the remote control. You look carefully at it as you press again. The little LED light doesn't come on. The battery must have run down. You press it one more time a bit harder just to make sure. Still nothing happens. You begin a search for batteries . . .

This little scenario illustrates a number of aspects of thinking. First of all there were a number of minor problems to solve: how to remove the cat hairs, where the brush was, what was wrong with the remote control, and so on. Second, solving them was fairly straightforward. You know how to clean cat hairs off furniture, you know where to find a brush, you know enough about remote controls to hypothesise why it didn't work. Third, the actions you undertook were goal oriented. The overall goal was watching TV with a glass of beer. The actions you performed were done to achieve that goal. Those actions were sub-goals, such as the sub-goal of cleaning the sofa to sit down to watch TV or the 'sub-sub-goal' of finding the brush to clean the sofa to sit down to watch TV.

The fourth point to note is that sometimes we lose track of where we are in a sequence of actions. In the scenario you returned to the living room without your beer. We can hold only so much information in working memory at one time. It is as if the sub-goals were stacked up in a pile with the currently active one at the top. Once it is 'satisfied' then it can be removed from the goal stack and the next one can take its place. If there are too many sub-goals then we may lose track of one or more of them or lose our place in the stack.

Life's more awkward problems

In familiar problems we generally know what we have to do – we have the relevant 'domain knowledge'. A **domain** is like a school or university subject (such as geometry or history) but can include any other area where some knowledge is needed (such as poker, or chess, or soap operas). By putting people in situations where they do *not* have the relevant domain knowledge we can observe how they use their intelligence, what strategies they use, how they cope with memory limitations, and so on. For that reason, the study of problem solving has tended in the past to deal with simple puzzle problems that the solvers have never encountered before and that, at first sight, seem to be irrelevant to everyday problem solving. However, although we don't spend much of our time doing wooden puzzles we do spend a considerable proportion of our lives doing novel problems in school that are just as puzzling. By starting from such simple problems psychologists have developed a vocabulary and methodology for examining more complex problem solving behaviour. For example: a student is studying psychology and has been given an essay about the role of reaction time experiments in cognitive psychology. The student knows nothing about the topic of the essay and she has two weeks to write it. All students are faced with tasks such as solving geometry problems, writing computer programs, translating passages of French, writing essays in domains they know little, or nothing, about. So what do you do when you don't know what to do? Well, to begin with, how you solve the problem depends on how you think of it. That is, thinking will depend on the mental representation you form of the problem in the first place.

Problem representation

Before going on, try to answer these questions:

(a) A man walks into a bar and falls on the floor. Why?
(b) How many members of each species did Adam take with him on the Ark? (Note that the question is how many members of each species rather than how many species.)

These two problems are, in fact 'garden path' problems. They are worded in such a way that the important or salient features (the features that would help you get the right answer) are deliberately obscured. There are many puzzles of this kind, often called 'lateral thinking' puzzles. They rely on the fact that the wording of the problem leads people to produce an inappropriate mental representation of the problem.

The reason the man fell on the floor when he walked into a bar was that it was an iron bar. In the second problem Adam didn't take anything onto any Ark – Noah built the Ark. It may be that you didn't solve the first problem at all. In the second, most people don't notice that 'Adam' is a salient feature. In both cases the wording of the sentences pushes the reader towards one interpretation (one mental representation) and away from another. People often walk into the kinds of bars where drinks are sold. It is the first meaning that will be accessed when the sentence is read and determines how the sentence is interpreted. Once an interpretation is formed it is often very hard to shift it. In the second problem attention was deliberately shifted from the name to the number of members of each species. The sentence in brackets emphasised this feature of the problem. Furthermore, Adam and Noah are semantically associated. If the question had asked how many members of each species the President of the United States took on board the Ark I suspect you would have noticed.

Neat procedures and cunning strategies

When the problem and its solution method are already known, in a sense you don't really have much of a problem: you just apply the solution method. When you don't have a complete representation of a problem, because the problem is unfamiliar, you have to rely on general methods that can be applied to a range of diverse problems. There are two classes of procedure (roughly speaking) for solving problems. There are often procedures that one can follow that are guaranteed to get a result. For example, suppose you wanted to follow a procedure that was guaranteed to complete any jigsaw puzzle. Such a procedure might be something like this:

1   Select at random a piece from the pile of jigsaw pieces and place it on the table.
2   If no more pieces are available, END.
3   Select at random another piece and check to see if it fits the first piece (or any other pieces that are successfully placed in the future).
4   If not, place it on a new pile (call it the discard pile).
5   Go to 2.
6   Once the first pile has been used up start again using the discard pile. Go to 3.
7   END.

A procedure such as the above is called an **algorithm**. Typical examples are computer programs and recipes. If they are written in enough detail and followed precisely they are guaranteed to work. Now you might realise that although the algorithmic method for doing jigsaws is guaranteed to work it would be excruciatingly slow. To do a jigsaw you would be more likely to fall back on problem solving strategies called **heuristics**. A heuristic is a rule of thumb that provides a way of going about doing something but is not guaranteed to work. Nevertheless, when you don't know what else to do heuristics are extremely useful and often quite powerful problem solving devices. Examples of heuristics for solving the jigsaw would be to pick out all straight edges, find the corners, find the pieces that refer to the same object in the picture or the pieces that are the same colour, and so on. While there are heuristics like those that are applicable only to one domain (e.g., jigsaws), there are also more general heuristics that can be applied in a variety of domains to solve a variety of problems.

One general problem solving strategy is known generically as **difference reduction** and involves trying to find some means of reducing the difference between where you are in a problem and where you want to end up. There are two main types: **hill climbing** and **means-end analysis**. Hill climbing is a metaphor for a type of thinking that involves taking one step at a time and seeing where it leads. If it leads 'uphill' – that is, it seems to be taking a step closer to the solution – then take that step, otherwise try taking a step in another direction.

If you are trying to listen to a radio programme in a car and the reception is poor you might press buttons or turn the tuning knob until you find the strongest signal. If you turn the knob and the signal gets stronger you keep going, since it seems to be reducing the difference between where you are and your goal. If the signal gets weaker then you start turning it back in the other direction, since you are heading away from the goal.

Try solving the following problem: three Hobbits and three Orcs want to cross a river. Unfortunately, the only boat available can hold only two creatures at most. Furthermore, if the Hobbits are ever outnumbered by the Orcs either on the boat or on the banks, the Orcs will eat the Hobbits. How do the Hobbits and Orcs all cross the river successfully and in one piece? Bear in mind that at least one creature has to be in the boat for each crossing.

In the course of solving the problem there is a point at which two creatures have to go back to the original bank (see Figure 2.1). Two Orcs are on the right bank (Figure 2.1f) and two Hobbits arrive to join them. The next step is for one of each to go back to the left bank (Figure 2.1g). This step seems to be leading away from the goal – it seems to be a step downhill. Taking two creatures back seems to be reducing, instead of

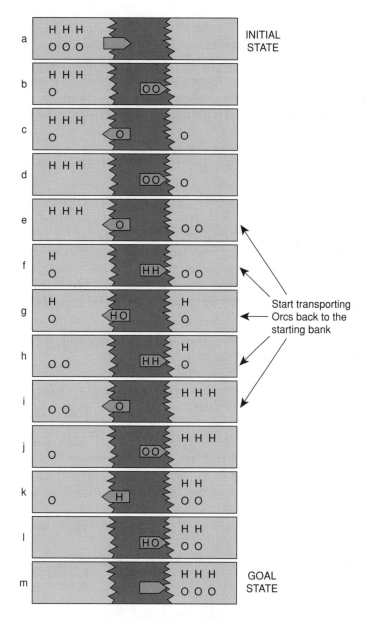

FIGURE 2.1 The solution to the Hobbits and Orcs problem
(H = Hobbit; O = Orc)

increasing, the number on the goal bank, and taking all Orcs to the goal bank and then taking them all back again seems on the surface a waste of time. Thomas (1974) found that people were reluctant to make this 'detour', and Greeno (1974) found that people slowed down and made most errors at this point.

Hill climbing is not a particularly efficient strategy. There is often no way of knowing whether the top of the 'hill' you have reached is the top of the highest hill. When you try to get a strong signal on the radio it may well be the best signal available, but without further search you have no way of knowing if there is a stronger one further along the dial. Still, if you are happy enough with what you can hear this would be an example of satisficing.

In problems where you resort to hill climbing, or even trial and error, there is often no obvious way of breaking the problem down into smaller sub-problems. It is not obvious, on first encountering the Hobbits and Orcs problem, that the first thing to do is get all Orcs from the left bank to the right bank. Problems can be made a bit more tractable if you can break them down into chunks or sub-goals. This is a more powerful difference-reduction heuristic known as means-end analysis. Using means-end analysis, solvers try to assess the difference between where they are now and where they want to be and work out what steps are needed to get there. If any of these steps is blocked (the sofa is covered in hairs) then set up a sub-goal to get rid of that block (get a brush). If any one of the steps in solving the sub-goal is blocked then set up another sub-goal to get rid of that block (can't find brush; search in likely places). Each time a sub-goal is achieved you are, hopefully, one step nearer your overall goal.

Problem structure and some limitations to thinking

Sub-goaling and means-end analysis have been studied using the Tower of Hanoi puzzle (see Figure 2.2), which has a relatively simple structure. It comprises three pegs fixed to a base board and a number of different sized rings that fit over the pegs. The

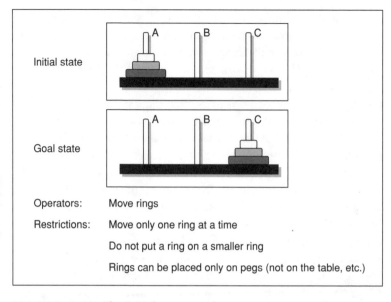

FIGURE 2.2   The initial state, goal state, operators and restrictions in the Tower of Hanoi puzzle

puzzle is usually set up such that all the rings are on one peg and the solver is asked to move them to another peg following certain rules. The way the puzzle is set up to start with is the **initial state** of the problem. When the rings have been successfully transferred to the goal peg the problem will be in the **goal state** (see Figure 2.2). In any problem whatever it is you can do to change the state of a problem is known as an **operator**. For example, there are the four arithmetic operators of addition, subtraction, division, and multiplication. Applying one of them changes the state of a problem. Thus the initial state might be $2 \times 2 = ?$ and by applying the multiplication operator you would get 4. These operators are actually **mental operators** – you have to do something in your head to get 4 from 2×2. If you were using a calculator to solve the problem then the operator would be to press a button, but it is still your head that tells your finger what to press. In the Tower of Hanoi there is just the one mental operator: 'move a ring'.

Another feature of problems is that there are often constraints or **operator restrictions** – things you are not allowed to do. In the Tower of Hanoi you are not allowed to move more than one ring at a time; you are not allowed to put a larger ring on a smaller one; you must move a ring to another peg and not put it on the table or in your pocket (Figure 2.2).

Constraints can either make things more difficult for you or make life easier. In Classical Greek drama and seventeenth-century French drama there were three 'unities' that had to be obeyed – the action of the play should take place over no more than 24 hours, the action should be in the same place, and the drama should be as plausible as possible. These constraints hemmed in French dramatists somewhat. Shakespeare and Goethe were not bound by them. Corneille's *Le Cid* had the hero winning the hand of his lover, fighting a duel with her father in which her father died, going off and winning a famous victory in a battle with the Moors, coming back and persuading his lover not to avenge her father – all in the space of a day. Not surprisingly Corneille was accused of violating the unity of verisimilitude (doing all that in one day is unlikely).

On the other hand constraints can make things easier if they reduce the number of choices you have to make. If you have to go from one town to another and it's too far to walk or take a bike and there is no direct train service or airport but there is a bus service and you have a car then these constraints may make a solution to the problem of how to get there easier.

The Tower of Hanoi problem, as it is set up in Figure 2.2, gives all the information you need to solve it. You know what the starting state is, what you are supposed to end up with and what you are allowed to do and not allowed to do to get there. It is therefore **well-defined**. In an **ill-defined** problem some information is missing. If I ask you for the third person singular imperfect subjunctive of '*avoir*' you may not have a clue what the question means. It is therefore ill-defined. If you do know what I'm talking about it is well-defined. Most problems we are faced with, such as writing essays, devising advertising campaigns, designing a new product, are ill-defined.

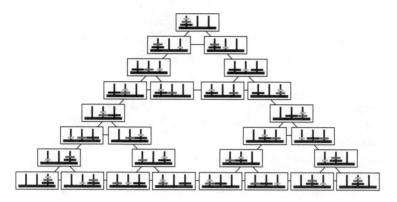

FIGURE 2.3   Problem space for the three-ring Tower of Hanoi problem

If you move the smallest ring in the Tower of Hanoi problem to the middle peg then you have changed the state of the problem. If you move the middle ring to the rightmost peg then you have reached yet another state. Using the information provided in the problem statement an all-knowing, perfectly rational problem solver can produce a diagram or map of all the possible states that can be reached in this version of the problem and can 'read off' the quickest route to the goal state. Figure 2.3 illustrates all the possible states you can reach in the three-ring Tower of Hanoi problem. The space of all possible states such as the one in the figure is known as the **problem space**. Newell and Simon (1972) proposed that thinking through a problem involved a search through such a problem space.

An example of this occurred recently when my 3-year-old daughter and I tried to assemble a device for drying pullovers. The dryer consisted of different coloured plastic tubes of different sizes along with connectors, corner pieces, netting and minimal instructions. We spent some time playing around with the parts, sticking them together and taking them apart. We were, in Newell and Simon's terminology, 'exploring the problem space'. As a result of this exploration putting the whole thing together eventually was very quick.

Newell and Simon took an information-processing view of problem solving where the solver is regarded as an information-processing system with certain limitations. By looking at problems in terms of problem spaces (particularly well-defined problems) you could compare how a perfectly rational system would solve the problem with what people actually do. The difference between the two tells us something about human psychology. What people actually do is affected by their limited capacity to process information, the contents and organisation of information in long-term memory, and the helpfulness of the environment (in, for example, directing our attention to relevant features of a situation).

One of the things that stops us from being perfectly rational is our limited capacity working memory: the bit of memory used for short-term storage and processing of information as explained in Chapter 1. Ordinary mortals can focus only on a limited part of the map and the surroundings are fuzzy since we can only cope with so much information at any one time. There are, however, ways of getting round these limitations.

Avoiding the limitations to thinking

As a result of the limitations of the human information-processing system we have developed ways of circumventing our limited capacity working memory and rely on our vast long-term memory. We do this in a number of ways. First, we can rely on and use constantly the kinds of general-purpose strategies (heuristics) mentioned earlier as 'this is the only way [we] can act appropriately within a reasonable time without thinking over the host of possibilities with all their consequences and all the possible consequences of the consequences' (Mérö, 1990, p. 72).

According to Newell and Simon (1972), the most important general strategy used by people lacking a perfect viewpoint is means-end analysis since it breaks problems down into manageable chunks. Another strategy for avoiding working memory limitations is to make sequences of actions as automatic as possible so we don't consciously have to think about them. Someone learning to drive a car has to keep track of a lot of information. A manoeuvre such as turning right involves checking the mirror, signalling, braking, pressing down on the clutch pedal, pulling the gear stick back towards you then across to the left and then towards you again; all while watching out for obstructions. The driver has to then slowly release the clutch while watching the road ahead and to the right, turn the steering wheel while replacing the foot on the accelerator. This is a lot of information for an inexperienced driver to process and can overload working memory, so the car stalls. However, the experienced driver has performed this and similar manoeuvres countless times and this practice has led to the actions becoming automatised and therefore to a reduction of the load on working memory. Shifting gear becomes a single 'chunked' sequence of actions rather than six separate ones. Practice allows a shift from controlled to automatic processing (Shiffrin and Schneider, 1977). The skilled driver relinquishes control to automatic processes and frees up working memory space to allow her to think of other things such as how to persuade that nice young man from the accounts department to go out to dinner with her.

A third strategy is to rely on simple associative learning mechanisms. We readily categorise objects, associating features with specific objects (wings with birds). We learn to do things that result in pleasurable outcomes and to avoid doing things that lead to unpleasant outcomes. We associate V-shaped fins sticking out of the water with sharks; someone might give up eating dry roast peanuts because they were once violently ill after eating them (although curiously they don't give up the red wine they had drunk in vast quantities at the same time). Dennett (1996) refers to this type of learning as ABC learning (for 'associationism, behaviourism, connectionism'). 'For many life-saving purposes (pattern recognition, discrimination and generalisation, and the dynamic control of locomotion, for instance), ABC networks are quite wonderful – efficient, compact, robust in performance, fault tolerant and relatively easy to redesign on the fly' (Dennett, 1996, p. 87).

A fourth strategy is to rely on cues provided by the environment. We can use some kind of external memory. Multiplying 368 by 473 is made relatively easy if you have a piece of paper and a pencil to keep track of where you are in the problem and intermediate results. We keep diaries, use Post-It notes, label things. We can also use the contexts and ready-made cues the environment provides to aid recall. If you have mislaid something you can go back to the place where you last had it and use the context to remind you what you did with it.

A fifth way to avoid having to work things out from scratch is to have a kind of ready-made 'inference engine'. With experience of events and relationships between objects or concepts we build a kind of structured mental representation that allows us to make sense of the interaction of objects or concepts in the world. Such a structured representation or framework for knowledge is often known as a **schema** (Rumelhert and Norman, 1985). A schema for a car, for instance, is likely to include several interrelated features. Schemas have 'slots' into which can be fitted fixed values (things a car has to have to be a car: fuel, engine, seats, wheels), default values (things you can assume a car has: locks, keys, disc brakes), and optional values (what a specific instance of a car has: three wheels instead of the default four). If someone is having a nice cappuccino you can make the default assumption that the cappuccino is hot rather than cold because your schema for coffee includes that information. Having a schema for an event, object or abstract concept helps us make sense of what is going on, guides what we pay attention to, and allows us to supply missing information unconsciously. In fact, the more information we can extract or infer from the environment the better able we are to survive in it.

Thinking with mental models

The first part of this chapter dealt with the fact that we generate a mental representation of a problem from information given in the problem and from memory. This is a mental representation that we build 'on the hoof', as it were. Schemas, on the other hand, are pre-stored mental representations derived from everyday experience and representing what things are like, what kinds of things happen in certain situations, and so on. However, sometimes our experience of the world provides us with the wrong mental representation of how things work.

For example, a person may have a rough idea of how a remote control works – some kind of beam of radiation comes out from one end and is picked up by some kind of receiver in the television. The beam and the LED on the remote control need an energy source provided by a battery. If nothing happens when the buttons are pressed then a possible reason may be that there is no energy source. The conclusion that the batteries need changing is therefore based on that person's **mental model** of how that person *thinks* the device works (Gentner and Stevens, 1983). A mental model is a mental representation of a device or state of affairs in the real world.

Naturally our mental models of how we think things work depend on our knowledge. Most people living in a technological society know how a remote control works well enough to use it. Fewer people would know how it works well enough to fix it. You may have a model of the device that varies in its 'opacity'; that is, for some people the workings of the device are opaque – they have no idea how it works. If their car breaks down they call a breakdown service. For others the workings are 'transparent' – they know how it works and how the parts interrelate. If their car breaks down then they are more likely to be able to fix it and carry on their journey.

The difference between these two mental models has been referred to as the 'black box versus glass box' distinction (DuBoulay, O'Shea and Monk, 1989). If you have a 'good' understanding of a remote control, the internal combustion engine, a computer program, a plumbing system, or whatever, then you are likely to have 'knowledge rich in relationships' (Hiebert, 1986). The richer the web of relationships, the better the understanding that derives from it, and the better able a person is to adapt that knowledge to new situations.

Halasz and Moran (1983) looked at what happens when you give people a 'glass box' view of a device by providing an appropriate mental model (a **device model**). One group of subjects was taught step-by-step procedures for solving problems using an early form of calculator called a 'stack calculator' (this was when electronic calculators were still a novelty). A second group were taught the same step-by-step procedures but were also given an explicit model of how the calculator worked. Both groups were then given routine and novel problems and asked to talk aloud while solving them. Both groups did equally well on the routine problems, but for novel problems the group who had been given the device model performed significantly better. From the think aloud protocols the researchers found that the group who had the device model used a problem space based on how it worked whereas the other group used a problem space based on recombined bits of known procedures. Providing a mental model for a system can therefore enhance understanding of the system and hence problem solving.

The same pattern of results was found by Kieras and Bovair (1984) who gave one group a set of instructions to learn by rote and gave another group a device model. The model group learned the instructions faster, were better able to remember them, executed them faster, and could adapt the procedures more often than the rote group. Schumacher and Gentner (1988) found that giving subjects a device model not only helped them learn the device quicker but also allowed them to transfer that learning to another similar device.

What this research shows is that a 'deep' understanding of systems allows more flexible problem solving than simply learning a procedure which provides only a 'surface' understanding of how something works. Learning about the underlying principles allows you to see why the procedures work and consequently how they might be adapted. If you know *why* a recipe works then you are more likely to be able to adapt it or even improve it.

The naïve physics of *Star Trek*

A system does not have to be all that complex for our mental models to be wrong. We can have faulty models of very simple

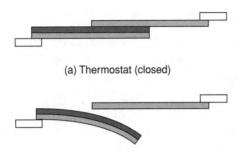

(a) Thermostat (closed)

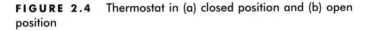

(b) Thermostat (open)

FIGURE 2.4 Thermostat in (a) closed position and (b) open position

devices such as thermostats. In fact even our understanding of what happens when something rolls off a shelf can be wrong. Such faulty mental models of everyday physical systems come under the heading of **naïve physics**.

A thermostat is essentially a simple device comprising a bimetallic strip that bends when it heats up. This bending causes it to break contact with an electrode ((b) Thermostat (open), Figure 2.4), causing the device to switch itself off.

According to Kempton (1986), people tend to have one of two models of how their central heating thermostat regulates the heating on their house. According to the *feedback model* the thermostat turns the central heating boiler on and off depending on the room temperature. Thus the length of time the boiler is on controls the temperature. Turning the thermostat up increases the amount of time the boiler is on for and therefore heats up the house. This is the technically correct model. According to the (incorrect) *valve model*, the thermostat acts like a tap and controls the rate of heat production in the boiler rather than the time it is on. Turning it up gives more heat. In 1986 Kempton argued that the wrong valve model used by up to 50% of people at least some of the time may be costing the US $5 billion per year in wasted heat.

Mental models of motion

Much has been written about the physics of *Star Trek*, but the writers tend to stick to the physics of faster-than-light travel, or matter transportation at the speed of light. Little has been said about the naïve physics of *Star Trek* based on medieval models of physics. During one episode, two of the crew of the starship *Enterprise* find themselves on board a shuttle with a faulty engine. Fortunately, Jordi, the ship's engineer, is one of them. He succeeds in getting the engines to start but they fail almost immediately. On the screen we see the shuttle start to move against a background of stars and then slow down and come to a halt again. Some people might notice nothing wrong with the shuttle slowing down when the engines fail. Cars slow down when we take our feet off the accelerator; but what causes the car to slow down? The answer is friction and air resistance. What, then, causes the shuttle to slow down given that there is no friction and no air in outer space?

From the days of Isaac Newton it has been generally known that objects in motion remain in motion in a straight line unless some force acts on them to alter that motion. Similarly, objects at rest remain at rest unless some force acts on them. If there is an object, such as a starship, in space and a force, such as an engine, acts on it then the object will accelerate until the force stops acting on it. When the force stops acting on it then the object will continue moving at the speed it was accelerated to until some force causes it to slow down. The shuttle should therefore continue moving after the engines fail. Countless episodes involve the ship's engineer complaining that the engines can't maintain the speed they are travelling at. The ship's engineer shouldn't complain about maintaining a 'speed' but rather about maintaining an acceleration. When the captain calls 'Full stop!' does he mean the engines should stop, bearing in mind that their relative speed will be maintained? Does he mean 'reverse thrust' to slow the ship's movement? But then when would the ship 'stop' – relative to the last planet they visited two weeks ago? In fact, 'full stop' doesn't actually mean anything in these circumstances.

The captain, Jean-Luc Picard, has the wrong mental model of how his starship works. Worse – so does his chief engineer.

Caramazza, McCloskey and Green (1981) found that many people had a mental model of motion that accorded with the medieval 'impetus theory' of motion, whereby the act of setting an object in motion imparts a force (impetus) that serves to maintain that motion. Over time the moving object's impetus gradually dissipates. Thus the shuttle's engines imparted 'impetus' to the shuttle which quickly dissipated causing the shuttle to slow down and 'stop'. In Figure 2.5 a ball travels along a surface at (a). Assuming no wind or air resistance the ball will continue its forward motion and be pulled down by gravity on leaving the surface, so what actually happens is shown in (b). The path of the ball will therefore trace a parabola. Subjects however tended to choose either path (c), where the ball eventually drops in a straight line, or even (d), where the ball continues briefly straight ahead before curving and dropping in a straight line. I had intended to call the latter the Tom and Jerry model of motion but Steven Pinker (1998) got there first with the Road Runner theory of motion. Cartoon characters often run off the tops of cliffs, come to a sudden stop several feet from the edge, feet still running in the air. After a moment they look down, look up,

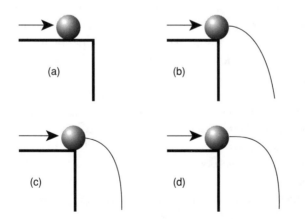

FIGURE 2.5 Predicted trajectories (b, c and d) of the ball in (a)

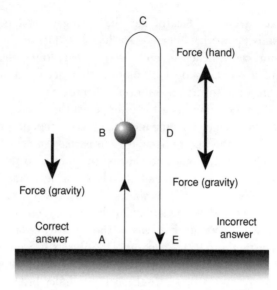

FIGURE 2.6 Correct and incorrect answers to the coin problem
(Source: Clement 1983)

gulp, and plummet. In both (c) and (d) the forward movement has somehow 'dissipated'.

The same phenomenon was described by Clement (1983), who referred to the impetus theory as the 'motion implies a force' preconception. Clement used problems similar to those used by McCloskey and his colleagues (1980), such as the coin problem (Figure 2.6). A coin is tossed at point A straight up into the air and caught at point E. Students were asked to draw arrows showing the direction of each force acting on the coin when it reaches point B. The correct answer is that shown on the left of the figure. Gravity is the only force acting on the coin after it leaves the thrower's hand. A typical incorrect response is shown on the right where there is some kind of 'force from your hand' (Force (hand)) which persists for a while before presumably dissipating as gravity takes over.

McCloskey, Caramazza and Green (1980) also found that about half their subjects believed a 'curvilinear impetus' could be imparted to an object (see Figure 2.7). Here the spiral movement

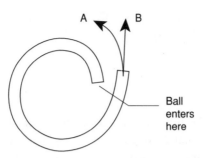

FIGURE 2.7 Ball enters spiral tube: 51% of subjects predicted that the ball would follow path A on exiting

of the ball round a spiral tube is maintained when the ball comes out of the other end. Again this movement is somehow dissipated since the path of the ball is presumed to 'straighten out' eventually.

These faulty models of motion seem to be maintained despite (or perhaps because of) our experience with the world and despite having some background in physics – even up to first year at college level. Furthermore, people are very good at giving plausible explanations for the predicted motion of the ball.

If you throw a ball in the air it continues upward once it leaves your hand as if the force imparted by your hand is still with it, at least that's what it *looks like*. The way Jean-Luc Picard thinks of the motion of his starship is the same way we think of the motion of our cars. Take your foot off the accelerator and they slow down and stop and there's a whole world out there that it stops relative to. We have to keep our foot on the accelerator to maintain a car's speed, and so on. The way we think of physical systems is therefore based on the analogies that we readily make (see Chapter 3).

Mental representations of devices, of situations and of physical laws have a powerful effect on the paths our thinking takes and on our behaviour. We make predictions on the basis of these mental models which can lead to error if the models are faulty. Nobody could have reached the moon who had an impetus theory of motion. On the other hand accurate mental models make learning and troubleshooting easier and help us transfer our learning to other similar situations.

Summary

Problems can be mundane or effortful. Mundane thinking uses well-known familiar strategies for coping with familiar problems. Effortful thinking is needed when problems are unfamiliar.

The quality of our thinking is based on:

- how good our mental representations are;
- how much load there is on our limited capacity processing system;
- how readily we can retrieve information from long-term memory;
- our relevant **domain-specific** knowledge.

Problem solving can be understood as a search through a problem space generally under the control of (**domain-general**) problem solving strategies called 'heuristics' of which the most general and flexible is means-end analysis, which incorporates both difference reduction and sub-goaling. Awkward problems are generally broken down into more manageable sub-problems (sub-goaling). This works both for well-defined problems (where the information necessary for its solution is given) and for ill-defined problems (where the solver has to provide missing information about possible solution methods and relevant information). In ill-defined problems the search for a solution is often a search for constraints that allow the problem to be cut down to manageable proportions. In essay writing, for example, this might involve deciding which examples to use, which aspect of an issue to discuss, and so on. Well-defined problems can sometimes be mapped out to show the entire state space. The state space does not necessarily determine the difficulty of the problem. Chess has a problem space with billions of possible states.

Solving problems can be made easier through practice, experience, and by relying on information provided by the environment. Nevertheless, despite our familiarity with everyday devices and physical forces, we sometimes build the wrong mental model of how these objects and forces work, mainly through faulty analogies.

Further reading

Gentner, D. and Stevens, A. L. (1983) *Mental Models*, Hillsdale, N.J.: Lawrence Erlbaum Associates. Contains a collection of papers on how various systems can be mentally represented.

Kahney, H. (1993) *Problem Solving: Current Issues* (2nd edn), Milton Keynes: Open University Press. Part I gives a clear introduction to information processing accounts of problem solving.

Chapter 3

Creative
thinking

Discovery consists of seeing what everybody has seen and thinking what nobody has thought.

(Albert Szent-Györgi von Nagyrapolt, *Science Needs Freedom*)

THE KINDS OF PROBLEMS DISCUSSED IN the last chapter involved working your way through them until you reach your goal. In these problems you usually have a rough idea where you are in the problem and often how close you are to the end. Another type of problem is one where you don't know where you are in the problem until an answer suddenly pops into your head and you shout 'Aha!' This is insightful thinking and is generally associated with creativity. One form of insight is suddenly noticing similarities between things that you (or perhaps nobody) had ever noticed before. Insightful thinking can be mundane – 'Aha! Now I see why this drawer is sticking!' – or of some greater significance – 'Aha! Now I see why the speed of light is constant irrespective of the relative motion of the observer!'

This chapter examines the nature of creative and insightful thinking. Are they different from other forms of thinking such as those already discussed? Are only geniuses truly creative? Can creativity be measured?

Sometimes creative leaps are made that link something in one domain (households, say) with a situation in an entirely different domain (daydreaming). The unexpected insightful link between two disparate domains underlies such things as the metaphors used in poetry or jokes. Hence a mapping of the two domains above would yield something like: 'The light's on but there's no one at home.'

Metaphors are a type of analogy and analogies can have a strong influence on how we understand new information and hence how we think about it. Analogies work when the relationships between objects in one domain are the same as those between different objects in another domain. Atoms and electrons are different from the sun and planets but the latter can be used as an analogy for the former since they both share the relation 'revolve around'. Analogies also work only when we understand the underlying structural features of at least one of the situations being compared. The light being on refers to signs of life, but since no one is at home then someone's thoughts are elsewhere. If you don't get below the surface features the analogy is meaningless.

Creative, insightful, analogical thinking tends therefore to involve breaking free of a current representation to see things in a new light.

Breaking out of a faulty representation

I once bought a box of envelopes and stuck address labels on to the front of each. When I came to put letters into them, I discovered that one edge of each envelope had been glued down so that the letter no longer fitted into the envelope. I was therefore obliged to pull each envelope slowly apart at the risk of tearing it so that I could fit the folded letter into the now crumpled envelope. After putting half a dozen letters into envelopes in this way I suddenly realised what I was doing. I then proceeded to put an extra fold into the letters at the side so that the letters now fitted into the envelopes without any problem. The moral of this tale is that studying human problem solving doesn't stop you from doing stupid things.

Whereas past experience is necessary, useful and relevant about 99% of the time, sometimes it leads us astray. Shopping in a large supermarket would take far longer if you couldn't rely on your past experience of where certain categories of goods are kept. In this case, however, past experience temporarily blinded me to a proper examination of the relatively simple problem of getting sheets into envelopes.

Insightful thinking involves breaking free of an inappropriate representation that prevents us from seeing the solution. My blindness to the structure of the problem of putting letters into envelopes lasted minutes. There have been examples of inappropriate thinking that have lasted for hundreds if not thousands of years. In the fourth century BC, Aristotle espoused both the view that the earth was the centre of the universe (the geocentric view) and the view that the circle was the 'perfect' shape. The sun, the moon, the fixed stars and the wandering stars (the planets) revolved round the earth in circular orbits. This view became fixed and prevented astronomers from seeing that there were other possible models of how the universe works. They became 'set' in their thinking.

As astronomers took more and more careful observations and measurements of the heavens, however, some anomalies cropped up. Some of the planets seemed to stop revolving round the earth and even to go back in the opposite direction briefly before continuing on their path. To fit these observations into a representation that had the earth at the centre of the universe and everything else moving in perfect circles, the idea of 'epicycles' (circles within circles) was invoked to explain the strange motion of the planets. This model of the universe was elaborated by Ptolemy in the second century AD.

The geocentric view of the universe lasted for 2,000 years despite being wrong. In the sixteenth century Copernicus placed the sun at the centre of the universe, thereby generating a model of the universe that explained a lot more than the Ptolemaic system. However, Copernicus was really concerned that aspects of the Ptolemaic system compromised the notion of having heavenly bodies moving in perfect circles and a heliocentric (sun-centred) system made it easier to use circles to describe orbits. So the Copernican revolution was still based on a faulty representation of the universe. It was Kepler some 60 years later who argued that elliptical orbits were the only way to explain the measurements of the moon and planets – a discovery Kepler was not pleased about 'Who am I, Johannes Kepler, to destroy the divine symmetry of the circular orbits!' (quoted in Koestler, 1970,

p. 208). Indeed, there may be great resistance to new ideas or alternative representations of a problem:

> to undo a mental habit sanctified by dogma or tradition one has to overcome immensely powerful intellectual and emotional obstacles. I mean not only the inertial forces of society; the primary locus of resistance against heretical novelty is inside the skull of the individual who conceives of it.
>
> (Koestler, 1970, pp. 208–209)

Not only do we get stuck in our mental ruts but, as Koestler points out, society has to be ready to accept any new revolutionary view anyone dares to put forward in science and the arts, from Superstring theory to half-sheep in formaldehyde. Galileo paid with his life for blatantly daring to go against received wisdom.

So what is creativity and what processes are involved?

The nature of creativity

Most definitions of creativity emphasise the products of creative thought. Creative products have two important features: they should be novel and they should be valuable or useful either to the person who created the product or to the culture into which it was created. Margaret Boden (1992, 1996) has called the first of these two senses **psychological creativity** or **P-creativity**. *(H-Creativity)*

Suppose you are making a cake and as you go about the messy business of separating eggs it suddenly occurs to you that a deep spoon with a hole in it would be the perfect device for allowing eggs to separate into the yolk and white without all the mess of pouring back and forth from one half of the shell to the other. If you had never seen such a device before then the invention would be 'psychologically creative' as far as you are concerned. You wouldn't make much money out of it, however, since it has been invented before. In this latter sense the creative product of your imagination, of which you are justly proud, is not **historically creative** (**H-creative**). To be historically creative the novel product would have to be one that had never been seen or thought of before. The second aspect of a creative product is that people should value it or find it useful in some way. A painting such as Van Gogh's *Sunflowers*, a song such as 'Candle in the Wind', a symphony such as Beethoven's Ninth, a device such as a printing press, a film such as *Casablanca*, are creative products that are appreciated by the culture into which they were born.

The source of creative products (creative thinking) has traditionally been viewed as involving some form of inspiration. Sudden flashes of insight, such as Archimedes' Eureka experience when he suddenly realised how he could find out how much gold was in a crown, solutions that come to people in dreams, and the nature of genius are all somehow ineffable. Inspiration strikes only some special people: Pablo Picasso, Leonardo da Vinci, Jane Austen, Albert Einstein, Charles Darwin, Elizabeth Frink are not as other mortals.

This view has been vehemently challenged by many psychologists, computer scientists and philosophers. Lamb (1991, p. 6), for example, has referred to it as 'crude and counter-productive'. Weisberg (1986, p. 3) argues that: 'If creative achievements ... come about through great leaps of insight, brought about by extraordinary thought processes, in individuals who possess some unanalysable quality called genius, then little more can be said.'

However, a lot more can be said.

Behaviourist psychologists in the middle of the twentieth century were not interested in creativity. John Watson, an early behaviourist, dismissed it out of hand. Either a creative product was a generalisation of something old so that it seemed new or it was produced by accident (Watson, 1958). The study of creativity was left to psychometric psychologists who were interested in the measurement of abilities such as IQ, personality, and so on, and Gestalt psychologists who extended their psychology of perception to the psychology of problem solving. One method was to examine the lives and works of creative individuals (e.g., Cattell and Drevdahl, 1955; Roe, 1952; and more recently

Eysenck, 1995; Gardner, 1993). The autobiographical approach produced anecdotal accounts of stages in creative thinking. Wallas (1926) listed these as *preparation, incubation, illumination* (also called 'inspiration' or insight) and *verification* (these are looked at in more detail on pp. 44–53). While Wallas was interested in the processes involved in creative thinking, for other researchers the question was what makes one person creative and another one not? For them, creativity was seen as involving a number of measurable traits just as personality was often seen as being composed of a set of personality traits. In particular, Guilford (1950) proposed two general types of thinking: **divergent thinking** and **convergent thinking**. In convergent thinking the thinker is expected to 'converge' on the appropriate answer to a problem. Convergent thinkers prefer problems that have a single correct answer. Divergent thinking involves producing a variety of possible answers to a problem; thus divergent thinkers prefer open-ended questions that allow for a range of novel answers. Such people are therefore creative individuals. Since IQ test questions tended to favour convergent thinkers, creativity tests were produced to measure divergent thinking. Examples of questions designed to measure creativity are listed below (see Torrance, 1966):

1   Suppose that all humans were born with six fingers on each hand instead of five. List all the consequences or implications you can think of.
2   List as many edible, white things as you can in 3 minutes.
3   List all the words you can think of in response to *chair*. (Give yourself 3 minutes.)
4   List all the uses you can think of for a *clothes hanger*. (Give yourself 3 minutes.)

People who produce many responses to questions such as questions 1 and 3 above were *fluent* thinkers. Counting the number of unexpected or uncommon answers amongst the responses gave an indication of the *originality* of a person's thinking. The more remote an answer was to the stimulus item the more creative or original the answer was deemed to be.

Creative thinkers were also *flexible* in their thinking. One measure of this is the number of times someone switches categories in response to an item.

Another aspect of creativity that Guilford believed was important was the ability to recognise that there is a problem in the first place. Recognising problems is known as **problem finding** (see Getzels, 1975). Many of us are familiar with those mail-order catalogues filled with solutions to problems you didn't even know you had.

Despite attempts to measure creativity in the same way as one measures abilities or personality traits, a clear relationship between such measures of creativity and creative accomplishments in real life has not always been found. That is, divergent thinkers may not be H-creative. Okuda, Runco and Berger (1991) found that problem finding was more predictive of creative accomplishments than other measures of creativity such as divergent thinking.

Another way of examining creative thinking is to treat it as a kind of special case of everyday thinking or problem solving. Johnson-Laird, for example, has likened creative thinking to learning.

> When you learn a new task, you assemble existing skills into a novel arrangement that meets the constraints of the task. When you create a new idea, you assemble existing elements into a novel arrangement that meets the constraints of the task. The difference between the two is that when you learn, you absorb information from a teacher or the environment; but when you create, the essential constraints are those you provide yourself.
>
> (Johnson-Laird, 1988, p. 257)

The 'stages' of creative thinking

Studies of scientific discovery and artistic production often show a slow development of the creative product. It is only after long familiarisation with the problem that a final result emerges or before there is any 'illumination'. And after the illumination the creator still has to check that the resultant creative product, whether it be an artefact or an idea, is what he or she is looking for. For convenience, we will look at the development of a creative product in terms of Wallas's four stages of preparation, incubation, illumination, and evaluation.

Preparation

Simon (1966) argued that the biographies of famous scientists showed that there was often considerable trial-and-error search through a vast space of alternative hypotheses before there was any breakthrough. Boden (1992) referred to this space as a *conceptual space*. Sometimes the exploration itself is the goal; at other times the goal is either unknown or only vaguely defined. Weisberg (1986) gives the example of the creation of Picasso's *Guernica* and of Crick and Watson's path to the discovery of the structure of DNA. Picasso produced and kept many preliminary sketches as he tried to home in on the final version. He was exploring the conceptual space, although not in this case a scientific one.

One of the results of an initial familiarisation and exploration of the conceptual space is working out what the constraints are. Crick and Watson made several attempts to build a model of the DNA molecule with two strands, three strands and four strands, and with the bases on the inside and on the outside. Most of these models were not viable, there were constraints that disallowed combinations of elements (how the bases connect, number of strands, amount of water present in the molecule, etc.). Often these constraints were pointed out by other people. This combining, deletion and reworking of elements is also evident in Picasso's sketches for *Guernica*. Each recombination then underwent some kind of critical analysis to produce the next version.

Looked at in this way, the early stages of the creative process are no different from any other type of problem solving that involves a search through a problem space. There are often intermediate solutions that have to be evaluated in the light of new constraints that emerge which may eliminate non-viable solutions; indeed the process often involves finding out what the constraints are.

Incubation

Now it may be that this exploration of the conceptual space, with its combining and recombining of ideas, doesn't seem to be leading anywhere. When this happens there is anecdotal evidence of a stage of incubation: the problem is left alone for a while and later, in an unguarded moment, the solution 'pops' into one's head. It seems as though some kind of unconscious thinking must be going on while the person is consciously engaged in some activity unrelated to the problem. The mathematician Poincaré claimed to have suddenly realised that some arithmetic problems he had been working on were related to non-Euclidean geometry. This happened as he was strolling by the seaside having given up the arithmetic problems in disgust. Kekulé claimed that the structure of the benzene molecule on which he had been working and getting nowhere came to him as he was daydreaming. Is there any more tangible evidence for this, however?

Silveira (1971, cited in Anderson, 1995) tested the effect of incubation on problem solving in a laboratory experiment. A control group (Group A) worked on an insight problem such as the one shown in Figure 3.1. After half an hour 55% found the solution. Group B did the same problem but were interrupted by a half-hour break before returning to the problem: 64% found the solution. Group C were given a 4-hour break in the middle of solving the problem and 85% of them successfully solved it.

Weisberg (1986), however, argues that laboratory experiments show mixed results and that overall there is little evidence for unconscious processes at work in creative thinking. Nevertheless, there have been several attempts at explaining incubation. When we attempt to solve a problem we usually try to use procedures that have been used before, or try to tackle the problem in a particular way. This is usually a perfectly sensible thing to do. Nevertheless, once engaged on a particular solution method,

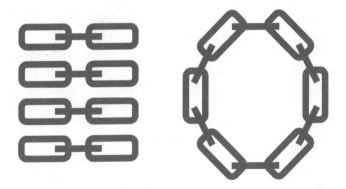

FIGURE 3.1 The chain puzzle

You have four separate pieces of chain that are each three links long. It costs 2 cents to open a link and 3 cents to close one. All links are closed at the beginning of the problem. Your task, should you choose to accept, is to join all 12 chain links into a single circle at a cost of no more than 15 cents. (See p. 141 for the solution.)

and if that method is inappropriate for the type of problem, we may get stuck in a kind of mental rut. We end up using an inappropriate **mental set** – our thinking gets set in its ways. Incubation means leaving a problem alone for a while so that the inappropriate sets get a chance to decay. When we get back to the problem later, a whole new way of seeing it may present itself.

Another explanation involves **spreading activation** (Yaniv and Meyer, 1987). Long-term semantic memory is like a vast network of interlinked concepts or 'nodes'. If someone is talking about an elephant and mentions that it lifted up a log of wood, we can infer that it lifted the wood with its trunk. We also know that elephants have tusks and big ears, are grey and are very large, that they are to be found in Africa and India and safari parks along with lions and zebras, and so on. We can access a lot of information relating to elephants and lots of information relating in turn to that information. Similarly, if you are trying to solve a problem, such as diagnosing a rash or being in an awkward position in a game of chess, then similar problems or contexts encountered in the past, along with procedures for solving them and so on, are likely to be activated. Those procedures may not be appropriate in a particular case but may, nevertheless, weakly activate information in long-term memory that is relevant to the solution. This weakly activated information is below a particular threshold level and so is not accessed during problem solving. Later, when you are no longer thinking about the problem, some accidental cue or hint in the environment may activate that weakly activated information causing it to breach the threshold level and an 'insight' will be experienced.

A third explanation of incubation was put forward by Simon (1966). The early preparation process, which Simon calls 'familiarisation' involves building a representation of the problem and storing relevant information about it in long-term memory. This information is used to generate new goals and sub-goals in working memory. During incubation there is 'selective forgetting'. The contents of working memory are volatile – switching attention can cause them to fade away – so when a problem is no longer being considered the goal information is lost. When the problem is later reconsidered this goal information has to be reconstructed, possibly using new data from long-term memory. A solver may therefore end up with a different set of goals and sub-goals, which may in turn reveal a faster solution.

Illumination (insight)

The incubation period often seems to come to an abrupt end with a sudden insight or illumination. Insight is perhaps a better term for this since it refers to an ability to see deep within a problem to its underlying structure. Wertheimer (1945) argued that people who try to solve problems, such as the ones shown in Figure 3.2, using their knowledge of geometry are using **reproductive thinking**. Reproductive thinking involves 'reproducing' learned solution strategies to try to solve the problem. Producing a novel solution to the problem was called **productive thinking**. Productive thinking requires an understanding of the deep structure of the problem.

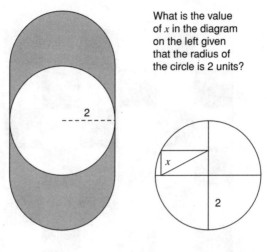

Imagine you have to paint around a circular window whose radius is 2 feet. You have a tin of paint that will cover 15 square feet. Do you have enough to paint the shaded area around the window?

What is the value of x in the diagram on the left given that the radius of the circle is 2 units?

(a)

(b)

FIGURE 3.2 Examples of problems used by Wertheimer (1945). *(See: p. 141 for answers.)*

Solving such problems was often seen as requiring insight – a light bulb lights up above your head, you raise a finger and say 'Aha!', you run naked through the streets of Syracuse shouting 'Eureka!', and so on. If your insight happens to be something no one else has ever thought before then it is H-creative.

Weisberg (1986) refers to the Gestalt view of insight as the ' "Aha!" myth', and many researchers have sought ways to explain insight and relate it to other, more 'usual', types of thinking. Generally speaking insight comes about when we switch attention from one aspect of a problem to another. As explained above, this may come about through weakly activated material becoming stronger or through selective forgetting.

Look, for example, at Figure 3.3. Suppose you had a chequer-board and 32 dominoes that fitted perfectly over two squares of the board so that they covered all 64 squares completely. Now imagine that the board was 'mutilated' by the removal of two squares in opposite corners. Can the remaining 62 squares be covered by 31 dominoes? Explain your answer.

FIGURE 3.3 The mutilated chequer-board

Solving this problem depends on the kind of representation you form of the problem. You might, for example, imagine trying to cover the board with dominoes in various configurations (this is the representation suggested by the problem). Kaplan and Simon (1990) refer to this representation as a 'covering' problem space. If you were mathematically inclined you might try to solve the problem mathematically. This would be a 'mathematical' problem space. If you looked for analogies then you would be searching through an 'analogy' problem space, and so on. The problem becomes one of finding a useful problem space in the first place

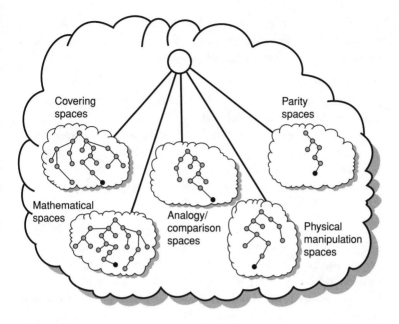

FIGURE 3.4 Representation of the different representations of the mutilated chequer-board problem

(see Figure 3.4). The solver has to search through the problem space of possible problem spaces. In studies of the mutilated chequer-board people began by searching for a solution involving covering squares with dominoes (the 'covering' problem spaces) which gets them nowhere. Eventually some tried to find a solution based on the fact that the dominoes had to cover two squares of different colours. This is the 'parity space' where the domino has to cover both a black and a white square. Once you hit on that problem space you realise that, if two black squares are removed then there will be two white ones that can't be covered.

Kaplan and Simon therefore argued that insight involves the same processes as other forms of problem solving; that is, a search within a problem space. Search within an inappropriate representation is unlikely to lead to a solution. Finding the correct representation often leads to a fast solution that gives the impression of 'illumination'.

Other researchers have linked insightful problem solving to everyday thinking and the limits to thinking. Ohlsson (1992), for example, argues that insightful problem solving involves:

(a) getting stuck;
(b) knowing how to solve the problem but not knowing that you know how to solve the problem;
(c) an 'Aha!' experience when the problem is re-represented in such a way that a solution becomes obvious – you suddenly realise that you do know how to solve the problem. A new representation of the problem makes available a new set of possible operators that may be relevant to the problem.

According to Weisberg (1995), people sometimes solve insight problems without an 'Aha!' experience; and sometimes people have a sudden 'mental restructuring' during non-insight problems. Furthermore, an insight may well be completely wrong. For this reason some kind of check is needed to see if the solution is viable; indeed, sometimes this evaluation takes years.

Verification and evaluation

Here is a 'lateral thinking' problem that one sometimes finds in puzzle books:

A famous thief in ancient China succeeded in breaking into the imperial palace and stealing three gold balls. As he made his escape the palace guard began to give chase. On the outskirts of the town the thief reached a rickety rope bridge. He had made his plans very carefully. He weighed 150 lb and each gold ball weighed 10 lb. However, the thief knew that the rickety old bridge could only support 160 lb. Once across to the other side he would be safe from pursuit from the heavily armoured palace guard. With a laugh he started to run across to the other side and managed to bring all three balls with him. How did he do it?

Once one has made some kind of creative leap and come up with some radical new idea, such as using clockwork to power a radio or using electricity to create light, one is often left with the problem of evaluating or verifying it. Einstein took some ten years to verify his insight into relativity. After some time thinking about the Chinese thief problem, puzzlers often come up with the traditional insightful answer that he juggled the balls. That way only one ball was in his hand at any one time. However, people often don't stop to evaluate this answer. You can't defy gravity that easily, since every action has an equal and opposite reaction. Using a force to throw a ball into the air produces an equal force in the opposite direction. If you don't believe me stand on a set of bathroom scales with a heavy book at waist height and watch what happens to the needle when you raise the book quickly up to shoulder height.

Verification can be a time-consuming and laborious process – sometimes an embarrassing one as Andrew Miles found out when he first demonstrated his proof of Fermat's Last Theorem, although he got it right in the end. A creative product also has to be evaluated by the society into which it is born. Unfortunately for the originator of the product, this may not happen in his or her lifetime. Painters of the Académie Française in the 1860s, such as Greuze and Gérôme, were more appreciated in their time than Degas, Renoir or Monet; but how many people today have heard of Greuze and Gérôme? 'If judgements of value can change with time, then judgements of creativity can change too. An act which is judged creative by one generation may not seem so to the next' (Hayes, 1989, p. 278).

Analogical thinking

Creative insights sometimes come about through someone realising that there is an analogy that helps them understand the problem they are working on. The power of analogies, including metaphors and similes in poetry and everyday language, lies in their ability to allow us to understand situations or problems in an entirely new way. **Analogical problem solving** means solving an unfamiliar problem in one domain using a familiar problem from another domain. Look, for example, at the 'radiation' problem originally used by Duncker (1945) to study insight:

> Suppose you are a doctor faced with a patient who has a malignant tumour in his stomach. It is impossible to operate on the patient, but unless the tumour is destroyed the patient will die. There is a kind of ray that can be used to destroy the tumour. If the rays reach the tumour all at once at a sufficiently high intensity, the tumour will be destroyed. Unfortunately at this intensity the healthy tissue that the rays pass through will also be destroyed. At lower intensities the rays are harmless to healthy tissue, but they will not affect the tumour either. What type of procedure might be used to destroy the tumour with the rays, and at the same time avoid destroying the healthy tissue?
>
> (Gick and Holyoak, 1980, pp. 307–308)

Gick and Holyoak (1980) used this problem in their study of analogical problem solving. The problem to be solved is known as the **target**. The analogy that is used to help solve the target is the **source problem**. Most people cannot solve the radiation problem without some kind of help; in fact, only 8% in Gick and Holyoak's 1980 study successfully solved it. However, when people are previously shown a source problem that has the same underlying structure more people are able to solve the radiation problem. The source problem used by Gick and Holyoak is known as the 'fortress problem':

> A small country fell under the iron rule of a dictator. The dictator ruled the country from a strong fortress. The fortress was situated in the middle of the country, surrounded by farms and villages. Many roads radiated outward from the fortress like spokes on a wheel. A great general arose who raised a large army at the border and vowed to capture the fortress and free the country of the dictator. The general knew that if his entire army could attack the fortress at once

it could be captured. His troops were poised at the head of one of the roads leading to the fortress, ready to attack. However, a spy brought the general a disturbing report. The ruthless dictator had planted mines on each of the roads. The mines were set so that small bodies of men could pass over them safely, since the dictator needed to be able to move troops and workers to and from the fortress. However, any large force would detonate the mines. Not only would this blow up the road and render it impassable, but the dictator would then destroy many villages in retaliation. A full-scale direct attack on the fortress therefore appeared impossible. How did the general succeed in capturing the fortress?

(Gick and Holyoak, 1980, p. 351)

The solution to the fortress problem is to split up the army (large force) into groups, and get them to attack (converge simultaneously on) the fortress (target). The solution to the radiation problem has the surgeon reducing the intensity of the rays (large force) and having several rays focus on (converge simultaneously on) the tumour (target). Armed with the fortress problem solution, but unaware that it had anything to do with the later radiation problem, about 20% of participants solved the target (radiation) problem. That's not much of an increase despite the fact that both problems employ the same 'divide-and-converge' solution schema. The number of successful solutions increased dramatically to over 90% when a hint was given to use the earlier problem when tackling the radiation problem. The hint forced participants to abstract out the relevant features of the fortress problem that would allow them to solve the radiation problem – roughly speaking those features that appear in parentheses in the two solutions above.

The power of analogical thinking

Analogies can have a powerful influence on thinking. In the 1960s and 1970s some countries in the Far East were likened to a row of dominoes waiting to fall under Communist control. If only one fell (Vietnam, for instance) the rest would fall inevitably one after the other. Freud's psychodynamic theory (and Tindbergen's theory of animal behaviour) took hydraulics as an analogy. Aspects of human behaviour were the results of pressure, in the form of psycho-sexual energy, building up in one place and finding a release somewhere else (in one's dreams, for example).

That said, several decades of research into analogical thinking has thrown up the somewhat counterintuitive finding that we are often very poor at using our previous knowledge to solve new problems. After all, only about 20% of the subjects in Gick and Holyoak's (1980) experiments spontaneously noticed the analogy. This is because the surface features of the problems – those aspects of a problem that are irrelevant to the solution – differed. One involved a dictator, roads, mines, villages, etc.; the other involved a surgeon, a patient, rays, a tumour, etc. Similarity of surface features is a strong determinant of whether an analogy will be noticed. Laser beams and 'rays' are more semantically related than armies and rays. So you might expect an analogy with a problem involving lasers to be noticed more than one involving armies (Holyoak and Koh, 1987).

Applying knowledge learned in one situation to a new situation is known as **analogical transfer**. However, even if something you have learned in one context is relevant to a new situation in a different context, using that knowledge is less likely. For example, what students learn inside school is often not seen as applicable outside school. The context exerts such a strong effect that the knowledge learned is not seen as being applicable anywhere else. The knowledge is said to be **inert** as it is tightly bound to the context in which it was learned and doesn't get called upon outside that context.

In a way, this serves to emphasise that remote analogies are 'creative' since they can be so hard to induce normally. Similarities between situations, such as trying to work out how much gold there is in a crown and having a bath, are few and far between, and hence not likely to be noticed. The similarities that do exist are in the deep structure of the problems and not in the surface details. A creative solution involves breaking free of a particular context in order to recognise the power of the analogy. Indeed, breaking free of a context or a representation or a traditional way of doing things is the hallmark of creative thinking.

Summary

The representation people have of a situation can have a profound and long lasting effect on thinking. It can take an enormous creative leap to overturn a well-worn representation and replace it with another.

While the lives of creative people have often been the subject of study it is only in the twentieth century that the processes underlying creativity have been studied. Some researchers regarded creativity as composed of traits similar to personality traits and IQ. Whereas IQ measured convergent thinking, creativity tests were supposed to measure divergent thinking and hence creativity. More recently, information-processing theorists have argued that creativity and insight are not essentially different from other forms of problem solving. Insight occurs due to breaking a mental set – a learned solution procedure (what the Gestalt psychologists called reproductive thinking) that is not helpful in solving a problem – or selective forgetting that allows a new representation to come about in which a solution seems obvious. There is also an important social or cultural dimension to a creative product. Creative products have to be seen as valuable or worth while in a society or else they are dismissed.

Analogies can sometimes allow us to re-represent a problem. Spontaneously seeing an analogy is often very difficult. However, when analogies are pointed out or used as an argument or explanation, or even in metaphors, they can have powerful effects on thinking.

Further reading

Eysenck, H. (1995) *Genius: The Natural History of Creativity*, Cambridge: Cambridge University Press.
Gardner, H. (1993) *Creating Minds*, New York: Basic Books.

There are many books on creativity and genius. Some tend towards the 'nothing special' point of view and others tend towards a natural history or psychometric point of view. For a balanced view the interested reader may like to compare Gardner's and Eysenck's books.

Logical and scientific thinking

LOGIC, n. The art of thinking and reasoning in strict accordance with the limitations and incapacities of the human misunderstanding.

(Ambrose Bierce, *The Devil's Dictionary*)

To what extent do we derive logically correct conclusions from the information we have? Is logical thinking something we learn how to do? This chapter deals with two forms of logical thought – deduction and induction – and discusses whether thinking changes in its nature as we develop. It looks at the extent to which children and adults can reason 'formally' and hence scientifically. The chapter also briefly examines some of the processes involved in learning from examples (induction).

One reason why our thinking is sometimes 'suboptimal' is that many of the circumstances that we evolved to cope with and to think about do not apply any longer for most of us. We did not evolve to unjam photocopiers, engage in hang-gliding, program computers, or operate hospital equipment that makes beeping noises. We evolved with the ability to invent tools such as spears, bows, boomerangs; to learn and automatise complex motor actions (for food preparation, for example); to learn languages (and hence to verbalise symbols and imbue natural phenomena with symbolic content); to make inferences from incomplete information.

Super (1980) describes the hunting abilities of a hunting and gathering society, the !Kung San of the Kalahari Desert. While hunting a giraffe they would search for clues such as the pattern of crushed grass, the colour of droppings, the blood on a bent twig 'evaluating the possible interpretations and their import for the hunt's final outcome; and planning a course of action' (Super, 1980, p. 61).

The blood on the broken twig, for example, could tell the hunters whether the giraffe is healthy enough to evade them for several days. This is the kind of reasoning that so impressed Watson in the Sherlock Holmes stories.

Development of thinking

Are we born with the ability to reason logically? Is it universal or culturally defined? In looking at these questions we have to ask whether children's thinking is qualitatively different from adult thinking (is it different in kind), or is children's thinking quantitatively different (is it a somehow 'simpler' version of adult thinking)?

The Swiss psychologist Jean Piaget was the first to study children's thinking in a comprehensive manner. He believed that thinking was our way of adapting to the environment. We either try to match information from the environment to what we already know or can do, or we adjust what we can do and what we know to cope with the environment. Since we know and can do different things at different stages in our development from babies to adults then our thinking is different at those different stages. At first the baby acts on the world through innate reflexes and responds to sensations. The adult can think about abstract ideas, make plans and generate hypotheses.

According to Piaget (e.g., Piaget, 1970; Piaget and Inhelder, 1958), intellectual growth is genetically programmed and more sophisticated types of thinking unfolded in a particular order given any reasonably rich environment. The quality of a person's thinking changes over time and comes about through the developing child's interaction with the world. In Piaget's first stage the baby's thinking is dominated by the influence of its sensations and its severely limited but gradually increasing ability to interact with the environment. This is the **sensorimotor stage** from birth to around 2 years when the child's thinking is limited to the immediate physical environment. The baby tries to incorporate new experiences into its existing very restricted repertoire of behaviours – innate reflexes such as sucking. Sucking behaviour is an 'action schema' that gets applied to almost anything that comes anywhere near the baby's mouth. Applying the sucking schema allows the baby to learn about the world and is the only mechanism available to the baby to do so. When new objects come near the mouth then they are sucked too. That is, the sucking schema is applied to all new objects coming near the mouth. Incorporating new objects into an existing schema is known as **assimilation**. If, on the other hand, a baby tried to suck a pin it would quickly come to realise that this new object does not fit readily into the schema. When experiences don't fit into pre-existing schemas then those schemas will either have to stretch to fit the new experience or new schemas will have to be created. This is **accommodation**. By interacting with the world in this way the child learns that its actions can have an effect and that objects in the world continue to exist whether or not the child can see them.

In the next developmental stage children can represent the world in words and images but the amount of manipulation they can manage is limited. This is the **pre-operational stage** from about 2 years to about 7. Children are beginning to learn to manipulate mental representations, although this ability is limited at first to the child's own point of view. They generally fail to do certain types of task at this stage. For example, they fail to conserve. Figure 4.1 shows two rows of marbles. When young children in the pre-operational stage are shown two rows of marbles laid out as in row (a) and then the marbles in one row are spaced out as in row (b) they typically say there are now more marbles in row (b) than in row (a).

Class inclusion also seems to pose a problem for children up to about 7 years old. If children of this age are shown a picture of flowers with six tulips and three daisies and asked 'Are there more tulips or more flowers?' they tend to reply that there are more tulips.

Why do they make these kinds of mistakes? Traditionally they are deemed to be fixing on only one perceptual feature or dimension of a task at a time. The row of marbles *looks* longer.

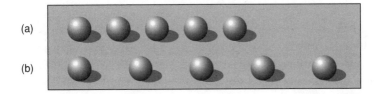

FIGURE 4.1   Conservation of number

In the flowers task the fact that there are more tulips stands out. Children focus on salient perceptual cues and ignore others because they don't yet know what property or properties of the situation are important.

Making mistakes on those problems in everyday life (say, when their brother ends up getting more Smarties than they do) eventually creates what Piaget calls **disequilibrium**. Something seems to be jarring in their understanding of the world. To adapt to the world the child will have to accommodate or assimilate new information to get back to equilibrium (a process known as **equilibration**).

The next stage is the **concrete operational stage** from 7 to about 11 years where children understand that quantities and volumes are conserved despite transformations. They can therefore go beyond the surface appearance of things and can classify objects along more than one dimension such as colour and shape. The child can now think through sequences of actions leading to a goal before (or without) performing them. Also the child now realises that some actions are reversible. What you can do you can sometimes undo. If you can add, then you can also subtract.

In the final **stage of formal operations** children become adults both physically and in their modes of thinking. The young adult can now engage in abstract thought: philosophising, hypothesising. The phrase 'formal operations' means the ability to perform logical operations on the contents of a mental representation. Thinking becomes more systematic and strategic. In the board game 'Mastermind' individuals at this stage should now be able to think through the deductive consequences of their choice of colours and positions and use strategies to get more information. Although this is the stage that Piaget believed that abstract and formal scientific thinking develops, some have argued that adults don't necessarily reach this stage (Gipson, Abraham and Renner, 1989).

Another way of looking at the difficulties children have on Piagetian tasks at different stages is to look at the nature of the tasks. It may be that these tasks were either misunderstood or simply made too many demands on an immature information-processing system (see Sternberg, 1990 for a brief review). As children get older their co-ordination improves, their fine motor skills improve, their knowledge of the world increases, and like-wise their information-processing speed and efficiency improves. Automatisation ensures that they don't have to rely on effortful processes to do complex tasks. For example, reading during the early years becomes easier and easier and therefore involves less effort. Improvements in knowledge and encoding information mean that children learn what aspects of the environment are relevant and should be attended to and hence encoded. Generalisation allows them to assume that toys that do things need to be switched on. Their general cognitive strategies improve. For example, they learn to rehearse items in short-term memory long enough to use them; they develop strategies for testing hypotheses: 'What happens if I press this button on mummy's computer?'

Although formal thinking is supposed to belong to the final stage of the development of thinking, very young children are capable of complex deductive inferences in situations that make sense to them. Thornton (1995) presents this example from a child aged about 2.

CHILD: (*Very aggrieved*) Jack broke my car!
MOTHER: I'm sure he didn't . . .
CHILD: He did! He did! Harry didn't go there [the play-room] – Jack broke my car!

The interesting point in this accusation is the clear and surprisingly complex chain of inference it involves: if the car is broken, then someone must have done something to break it; if someone broke the car, then they must have been in the playroom (where the car was) at the time. If Jack went into the playroom and Harry didn't, then only Jack could have broken the car, so he is the main suspect.

(Thornton, 1995, p. 14)

What subsequent work based on Piaget's theorising has shown is that he both underestimated the cognitive abilities of children and the role of knowledge in thinking and sometimes overestimated the abilities of adults (Donaldson, 1978; Siegler, 1998). Furthermore, context plays a strong role in reasoning. When the context is meaningful and familiar to the child the reasoning can be quite sophisticated. This is also true of adults, and we will now go on to look at this more closely.

Reasoning

The two main forms of reasoning that we engage in are deductive reasoning and inductive reasoning. **Deductive reasoning** is using knowledge that you already have to make an inference about some specific case. **Inductive reasoning** means generalising from particular instances. Inductive inferences are often the source of our general knowledge, which in turn is the source of our deductions. Another distinction between the two is that deductive reasoning involves deriving a *logically correct conclusion* based on a number of statements called **premises**. Any conclusions you reach in inductive reasoning on the other hand are only more or less probable, they are not logically certain.

Deductive thinking

Consider the following statements:

(a) All men are mortal
    The Prime Minister is a man
    Therefore the Prime Minister is mortal

(b) All dogs bark
     Cats are not dogs
     Therefore cats do not bark

(c) All men are mortal
     Margaret Thatcher is not a man
     Therefore Margaret Thatcher is not mortal

In (a) there are two assertions (or propositions) that are linked together to form the premises of a **syllogism**. The third line is a conclusion that must be true if the premises are true. In (b) we might not notice that the conclusion does not follow from the premises. It looks to be true since it fits with our prior knowledge of the world. However, the structure (the syntax) of the argument is actually identical to (c) whose conclusion conflicts with what we know and so we are more inclined to notice that the structure of the argument is wrong. Knowledge of the content of an argument can sometimes interfere with our ability to reason in this way despite the fact that deductive reasoning guarantees the correctness of a conclusion.

There are two aspects to deductive reasoning that are important. One is the form or syntax of the syllogism. A conclusion is either true or false based entirely on the syntax of the set of propositions. The other is the content. Any individual proposition may be either true or false. We tend to use our previous knowledge of the world when interpreting logical statements and this biases our reasoning, as we saw earlier. In Table 4.1 the syntax of the statements yields the conclusion irrespective of what A, B and C actually stand for. In other words, if you assume the premises, the conclusion *must* follow. Logicality and world knowledge are not the same thing.

The form of logical arguments has been used to examine whether people can infer consequences (e.g., all As are Bs; all Bs are Cs; what follows?). Quite often people make the wrong inference. The inferences in the middle column of Table 4.2 seem plausible but do not follow logically from the syntax of the argument. Compare them with their counterparts in column 3 (the symbol ∴ means 'therefore').

TABLE 4.1   Logically valid conclusions

All As are Bs	All daffodils are flowers	All canaries are birds
All Bs are Cs	All flowers are plants	All birds are blue
Therefore all As are Cs	Therefore all daffodils are plants	Therefore all canaries are blue

Column 3 in Table 4.2 contains the same structure of premises and conclusions as column 2 but the examples here are more obviously fallacious. Working out whether a conclusion is logically valid or not is tricky since it makes great demands on working memory. There are various theories as to what exactly those demands are and focus on whether our thinking is mainly rules-based (e.g., Bonatti, 1995; Rips, 1986, 1990) or whether we use mental models of the situations described in the Tables 4.1 and 4.2 (e.g., Byrne and Johnson-Laird, 1990; Johnson-Laird and Byrne, 1991). The greater the number of possible models that fit a situation the harder it is to work out what follows.

It is much easier therefore to rely on our general world knowledge. It is usually the case that if the argument looks correct it probably is correct. If a conclusion doesn't seem right then we would have to think about the structure of the argument. This general point is worth emphasising since it crops up in various guises throughout this book. The environment comes with a structure that we can use to guide our thinking. Likewise our past experience and world knowledge are extremely useful guides most of the time. If a conclusion fits in with that world structure or with our knowledge then chances are it's right. Certainly we would be more right than wrong to go along with it. The same general point applies for example to conditional thinking where we use 'if . . . then' rules.

TABLE 4.2 Logically invalid conclusions

Syntax	Plausible	Implausible
Some As are Bs	Some writers are women	Some writers are men
Some Bs are Cs	Some women are mothers	Some men are illiterate
∴ Some As are Cs	∴ some writers are mothers	∴ some writers are illiterate
No As are Bs	No logicians are stupid	No cows are fish
No Bs are Cs	No stupid people are fish	No fish are mammals
∴ No As are Cs	∴ No logicians are fish	∴ No cows are mammals
All As are Bs	All of the Frenchmen are wine drinkers	All vets are animal lovers
Some Cs are Bs	Some of the wine drinkers are gourmets	Some teachers are animal lovers
∴ Some Cs are As	∴ Some of the Frenchmen are gourmets	∴ Some teachers are vets

Conditional thinking

Consider the problem described in Figure 4.2.

Most people are not to be very good at getting the correct answer to this problem. Typical answers include turning over the card with the vowel alone, or turning over the card with the vowel and the card with the even number. Neither is the correct answer. Over the years many researchers have tried to suggest why the problem is so difficult given that the rule is so simple.

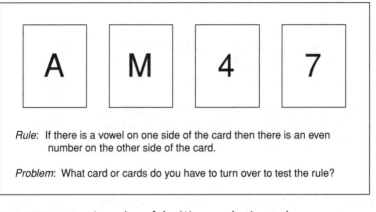

FIGURE 4.2 A version of the Wason selection task
(Source: Wason, 1966)

Now try the problem illustrated in Figure 4.3. Most people don't have much difficulty with the problem. However, it is identical in structure to the abstract version in Figure 4.2. Figure 4.4 shows how they map. For example, as a police officer you would want to check what the 15-year-old is drinking (this is equivalent to turning over the A card). The 45-year-old is of no consequence, she can drink what she likes. The person drinking lemonade is likewise irrelevant – anyone is allowed to drink lemonade. However, people often turn over the '4' card in the abstract version of the problem even though it is irrelevant to testing the rule. The fourth person is drinking beer so you would want to check his age (equivalent to turning over the 7 card which people very rarely do).

Concrete versions of the task that involve permissions, obligations and promises, such as the police officer version above, don't pose much of a problem for us. In those circumstances it seems obvious how to test the rule. Two reasons have been put forward for this. The first appeals to what are called pragmatic reasoning schemas, and the second proposes an evolutionary explanation, although the two theories can be seen as complementary.

Imagine you are a police officer and you have heard reports that there is under-age drinking going on at a local pub. You go in and at one table there are four people. The first is 15 years old, the second is 45 years old, the third is drinking lemonade, and the fourth is drinking beer.

Rule: If someone is under 18 they are not allowed to drink alcohol.

Problem: What do you have to check to see that the rule is being obeyed?

FIGURE 4.3   A concrete version of the selection task

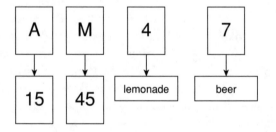

FIGURE 4.4   The abstract and concrete versions of the selection task

Pragmatic reasoning schemas

Cheng and Holyoak (1985) argued that certain contexts made the selection task much easier because the task fitted in with people's previously constructed schemas about those contexts. For example, we are familiar with contexts that involve permissions and obligations. According to Cheng and Holyoak we have schemas in the form of rules that involve a precondition of some kind. It is a precondition of drinking beer in a pub that you be over 18, for example. The rules look something like these (the parts within the < > represent slots that can be filled with specific values):

1   If <action is taken> then <precondition needs to be satisfied>
     If you want to drink beer then you have to be over 18.

2   If <action is not taken> then <precondition need not be satisfied>
     If you don't want to drink beer then you don't need to be over 18.

3   If <precondition is satisfied> then <action can be taken>
     If you are over 18 you can drink beer.

4   If <precondition is not satisfied> then <action can not be taken>
     If you are not over 18 you cannot drink beer.

These rules would lead people to choose rules 1 and 4 since they apply to the permission schema; that is, they state what the precondition for drinking beer is and what you are not allowed to do if you are under 18.

Evolutionary explanations

Cosmides and Tooby (1992, 1995) have proposed that the evolutionary history of the human species has made us very sensitive to reciprocity: you scratch my back and I'll scratch yours (see Ridley, 1997). The world is not a fair place: hurricanes aren't fair, famines aren't fair. Yet from a very early age children will complain that things are 'not fair'. Why should they expect them to be? Two of the human evolutionary strategies for survival are co-operation and division of labour on a massive scale, both of which require sensitivity to social exchange. Thus behaviours such as promising, trading, cheating are important for us as a species. Cosmides and Tooby argue that this makes us sensitive to reciprocity: we 'do as we would be done by' – and we don't like cheats. We are, therefore, innately equipped to think about forms of the selection task involving permissions and obligations that fit in with social exchanges (and incidentally helps explain our perennial fascination with cop shows on TV) but are poor at thinking about other forms of the selection task.

If you go down to the woods today . . .

The abstract form of the selection task emphasises its structure rather than the content. There is a huge number of situations that rely on the 'if . . . then . . .' structure of the selection task, so understanding the abstract structure is important. Rules, hypotheses, warnings and beliefs can often be stated in the form 'if . . . then . . .'. As with the syllogisms above they have a certain syntactic structure. A warning might be stated: 'If you go down to the woods today you're sure of a big surprise.' A rule might be 'If at first you don't succeed, try, try, try again.' Hypotheses including experimental hypotheses in science are of the form 'if . . . then . . .': 'If the car doesn't start and there is a spark from the battery then the fault might lie in the distributor.' An example of a belief might be: 'If God had meant us to fly he would have given us airline tickets.'

When you have a rule then you can often make inferences when you are given certain pieces of evidence. What follows (what inferences can you legitimately make) given the following rule:

> If I eat spinach I'll grow strong
> *Given*: I eat spinach; what follows?
> *Given*: I grow strong; what follows?
> *Given*: I don't eat spinach; what follows?
> *Given*: I don't grow strong; what follows?

There are two parts to a conditional rule: an 'if p' part and a 'then q' part. The 'if p' part is known as the *antecedent* and the 'then q' part is known as the *consequent*. As with the syllogisms mentioned above we can derive the truth or falsity from the structure alone. These will be clearer if we look at specific examples:

Rule:	IF p (If you go down to the woods today)	THEN q (you're sure of a big surprise)
Given:	p (You go down to the woods)	
What follows?		q (You get a big surprise)

Now assume that q is not the case.

Given:	NOT q (You don't get a big surprise)	
What follows?		

What follows from '(If you go down to the woods today)' is a tad tricky because the word 'if' actually means two things. In the simple sense, you might stay away from the woods and your car explodes. Getting a big surprise is not dependent on going down to the woods. In the second sense of 'if' you get a big surprise *if and only if* you go down to the woods. You can open a safe door if and only if you know the combination. Table 4.3 gives a list of conclusions that can be reached (some of which are invalid) given certain evidence. The truth or falsity of logical statements is not always easy to get to grips with, so the following discussion may require some careful reading (the symbol ∴ means 'therefore'). Table 4.3 gives the technical terms in the centre column but the main thing to look at are the types of valid and invalid conclusions. The inference: 'if p then q; p; ∴ q' (if p is

TABLE 4.3 Valid and invalid conclusions

	Rule	Example	Name
1	If p then q	If I eat spinach I'll grow strong	*Modus ponens*
	Given: p	Given: I eat spinach	Affirming the antecedent
	∴ q	∴ I will grow strong ✔	(valid)
2	Given:	Given: I don't eat spinach	Denying the antecedent
	NOT p	∴ I won't grow strong ✗	(invalid – no conclusion possible)
	∴ NOT q		
3	Given: q	Given: I grow strong	Affirming the consequent
	∴ p	∴ I eat spinach ✗	(invalid – no conclusion possible)
4	Given:	Given: I don't grow strong	*Modus tollens*
	NOT q	∴ I don't eat spinach ✔	Denying the consequent
	∴ NOT p		(valid)

true, then q is true; p is indeed true, therefore q must be true) is known as **modus ponens**. The inference: 'if p then q; not q; ∴ not p' (if p is true then q is true; q is not true, therefore p can't be true) is known as **modus tollens**.

Generally speaking, people are good at making valid inferences when told that p is true, but are not so good at making inferences when told that q is false. For example, when people are given 'not q' ('I won't grow strong') they might state that nothing follows.

Understanding how people think logically is extremely important. Getting arguments wrong can have serious consequences. Evans (1989a) pointed out that some of the arguments in a famous child abuse case at the time were in danger of being faulty. Consider the following:

> if someone sexually abuses a child then the child will display a positive response to a reflex anal dilation test;
> a child displays a positive response to a reflex anal dilation test;
> therefore someone has abused the child.

This is the invalid argument known as affirming the consequent (see Table 4.3). The conclusion depends on the likelihood and number of alternative explanations. The child may have been abused, but we cannot be certain as there are other reasons that can produce anal dilation.

In the Wason selection task people typically turned over the card that proved the rule (affirmed the antecedent) – this is *modus ponens*. To test the rule fully, however, they should also have used *modus tollens*. Only a tiny minority use both in the selection task. Indeed, it is a feature of human reasoning that we attempt to find evidence for a hypothesis, belief, prejudice, dogma or whatever and ignore or even disregard evidence that is likely to falsify it. This is known as the **confirmation bias**. There are lots of examples in politics.

If a government changes its policy on something it is usually 'accused' of making a U-turn. Margaret Thatcher famously claimed 'the woman's not for turning'. However, if a government has a policy that says that if we do p then q should happen and it turns out that q doesn't happen, what follows? Logically *not p* should follow. Actually what often follows is that policy p continues regardless because governments can't be seen to make mistakes despite the fact that a U-turn in circumstances where a policy is unlikely to work is a rational decision. Changing one's mind is a sign of 'weak' government:

> Some think that changing one's mind is a sign of weakness and that a good thinker is one who is determined,

committed, and steadfast. Such people, if they followed their own standards, would be more likely to follow their beliefs irrationally. Others believe that good thinkers are open-minded, willing to listen to the other side, and flexible. Most of us probably subscribe somewhat to both of these beliefs.

(Baron, 1994, p. 290)

Inductive thinking

Inductive thinking is something we are rather good at, especially as it is our main mechanism for learning about the world. Inductive thinking refers to the extent to which we can make reasonable generalisations from our specific experiences. When Alexandre Dumas *fils* said that 'all generalisations are dangerous, including this one', he was referring to the fact that generalising from experience is not guaranteed to give a correct answer. If I encounter thousands of examples of animals that swim in the sea and have fins and tails and each one I encounter is called a fish, I am likely to make the not unreasonable inductive inference that all animals that swim in the sea and have fins and a tail are fish; but I would be wrong. In fact, it takes only a single contradictory observation to make an inductive conclusion invalid. If I encounter a dolphin then my conclusion is wrong. I have to rely on likelihoods instead.

Nevertheless, induction is an extremely powerful thinking mechanism since it underpins almost all learning. It allows you to learn fairly quickly to make new types of inference that you have never made before. Suppose you are looking over the shoulder of someone working at a computer. You see her type in:

    car (a b c)

on the screen and then hit the ENTER key. The letter 'A' then appears on the screen on a new line thus:

    car (a b c)
    A

Unless you know something about the LISP computer programming language you may be completely baffled about what is going on. Suppose the computer operator now types in:

car (mother father uncle aunt)

and hits the ENTER key. Now the word 'MOTHER' appears on the next line. Now she types in:

car (daisy daffodil cornflower marigold hyacinth)

and asks you to guess what will happen when she hits the ENTER key. What would you say? She hits the ENTER key and the word 'DAISY' appears. She now types 'car (roof wall door)'. The screen therefore now looks like this:

car (a b c)
A
car (mother father uncle aunt)
MOTHER
car (daisy daffodil cornflower marigold hyacinth)
DAISY
car (roof wall door)

Can you now apply what you have learned from the first three examples to this new case? In fact in LISP the effect of typing 'car' followed by a list of items in parentheses is to print the first item in that list. If you managed to work out what would happen next (the computer would print 'ROOF') then you must have inferred some rule (or generated a hypothesis, to put it another way). In this case the inference is not based on anything you knew previously, assuming you knew nothing about LISP.

Gregory (1984) gives the example of Mendeleev who formulated the table of the chemical elements by inductive means. Mendeleev played a kind of game of patience in which the known elements and their atomic weights were written on cards, Mendeleev trying to find a systematic way in which he could lay them out in a pattern. The game resulted in a series of columns of seven cards, except that there were gaps. Several elements seemed to be missing, but their properties could be inferred from

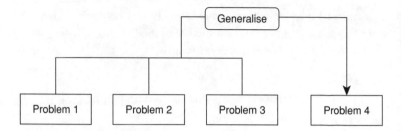

FIGURE 4.5 Experience of examples allows a generalisation to be made to other problems of the same type

the overall arrangement of cards. Through purely inductive reasoning and no other evidence 'he predicted with accuracy the properties of unknown substances which were later found. What more can one ask?' (Gregory, 1984, p. 244).

Induction can be extremely useful since it can give a basis for further thinking, and even testing if one is scientifically minded. It also forms the basis of much textbook learning where students learn to solve problems by looking at examples and solving other problems of the same kind. In Figure 4.5 three problems are generalised over and the resultant inductive inference can be applied to a fourth problem.

Conservative and liberal induction

Some types of inductive thinking appear to be rapid and effortless and others are somewhat slower and more effortful. Medin and Ross (1989) argue that we preserve a lot of specific detail about examples of a concept in case we make a mistake. Making sweeping generalisations can be dangerous. Instead they argue that **induction** *is* 'conservative' and that our knowledge contains much specific detail that may or may not be relevant to the concept.

> we argue that specificity may make access to and application of relevant knowledge easier, may permit more graceful updating of knowledge, may protect the cognitive system

from incorrect and inappropriate inferences, and may provide just the sort of context sensitivity that much of our knowledge should, in fact, have.

(Medin and Ross, 1989, pp. 190–191)

If this is the case then we would expect context to exert a strong influence over our ability to generalise and transfer solutions from one problem to another, or to categorise new examples of an object. If you are told that a shirkle is a bird with purple feathers and a yellow cross on its head then next time you see a bird with purple feathers and a yellow cross on its head you are liable to say 'Hey! Wow! A shirkle, as I live and breathe!' But suppose you see a bird with purple feathers and a white cross on its head. Is that a shirkle? Or what if it had dark blue feathers and a yellow cross? Conservative induction says that we have to be careful about just how far we can generalise from a limited number of examples.

However, there is a gradient from conservative to what one might call **'liberal' induction**. Some forms of thinking allow us to induce things very quickly indeed. There is a degree of structure in the world and we have evolved to deal with it. After tasting an unusual fruit and being violently sick it would be foolish to eat that food again. In this case we are quite happy to generalise from a single example. If our cognitive system made it difficult to learn from such experiences our species would not be around today.

Consider the following amusing example about the differences between English English and American English.

ENGLISHMAN: Lord Hutchins was my fag at Eton.
AMERICAN: Gee, you British sure are frank.

What is remarkable is that, from the single statement by the Englishman, the American happily generalises to all British people. And we don't notice. There seems to be nothing particularly conservative about the induction here. In fact some inductions can be frighteningly liberal. We often hear generalisations such as 'Men! Can't live with them, can't shoot them.'

Suppose someone – let's call him Albert – shoots Bob. Now imagine that Charlie gets very upset by this and so goes off and shoots Dave (who, by the way, knows nothing about Albert, Bob or Charlie). How would you make sense of this scenario? Charlie's behaviour does not seem to make any sense. Nevertheless, this is the logic of retaliation. Suppose Albert is a terrorist; Bob is a member of a different ethnic group or religion; Charlie is a member of the same group as Bob; Dave belongs to the group the terrorist claims to be fighting for. What didn't make logical sense now somehow makes human sense.

Conservative induction is a useful strategy in circumstances where there is some doubt about how to classify an object or situation. Natural objects such as animals and plants can be categorised more readily than 'unnatural' categories such as classes of algebra problems or problems in thermodynamics. The latter are not the classes of things humanity primarily evolved to deal with so learning about them can be effortful. Induction here should be fairly cautious. On the other hand, some aspects of thinking lead to a very liberal kind of induction that seems to be remarkably error prone.

We are very good at using information in the environment to make deductive and inductive inferences. We can make fast and generally accurate decisions when it counts. Indeed, it is a sign of our species' intelligence that we can use the environment in this way. Unfortunately, in many of the circumstances that face us in our current civilisation this 'intelligence' can at times be maladaptive.

Summary

Piaget believed that thinking unfolded in stages and that the types of thinking exhibited at any one stage were different from those at other stages. From an information-processing perspective, the development of thinking is linked to an increase in knowledge, working memory capacity, the ability to focus on more than one dimension of a situation at a time, and so on. Piaget also believed that formal reasoning was the final stage of development when children became capable of abstract thought and hypothesis testing. Garnham and Oakhill point out that:

> in one sense, deductive reasoning does not take us beyond what we already know. Inductive reasoning, in which, roughly speaking, we generalise from experience, does allow us to derive genuinely informative conclusions, but the result is that the guarantee of validity ... is forfeit.
>
> (Garnham and Oakhill, 1993, p. 128)

Our ability to reason deductively tends to be affected by context and the believability of our deductive conclusions. In other words, the surface structure of an argument interferes with our ability to reason using the underlying structural features of the argument. We also seem to be more innately predisposed to reason about some situations rather than others.

Inductive reasoning is a powerful learning and generalisation mechanism. The ease with which we can reason inductively depends on the context and the domain. In some cases 'one-trial learning' is enough to learn about something or a category of things. Liberal induction can be effortless and dangerous since it can easily lead to the wrong conclusions. Conservative induction means that we need to have experience of several examples of a category before we can be sure of the range of things a concept applies to.

Further reading

Evans, J. S. B. T., Newstead, S. E. and Byrne, R. M. (1993) *Human Reasoning: The Psychology of Deduction*, Hove, Sussex: Erlbaum. Presents very detailed coverage of deductive reasoning, but is rather heavy-going for the beginner.

Garnham, A. and Oakhill, J. (1993) *Thinking and Reasoning*, Oxford: Blackwell. Chapters 4–8 cover logic, deductive and inductive reasoning in some detail but in a readily accessible way. Chapter 16 also contains a description of Piaget's theory of the development of thinking.

Failures of
thinking

An error no wider than an hour will lead a hundred miles away from the goal.

(German proverb)

T HIS CHAPTER DEALS, UNFORTUNATELY, WITH failures of thinking. I say 'unfortunately', because dwelling on failures is likely to prejudice your thinking about human thinking. First impressions are hard to shake off despite later proof that they are wrong. So despite whatever I may subsequently say about how ingenious humans are, how fast and accurately they make decisions, how noble in reason, how infinite in faculty, in apprehension how like a god, the things that go wrong with human thinking are likely to stick in your mind because that's what this chapter concentrates on.

In fact, several 'failures of thinking' have already been discussed. Chapter 1 pointed out that rationality was bounded because of certain processing limitations to our thinking. Chapter 2 discussed the effects of having a faulty or incomplete mental representation of a problem situation. Chapter 3 referred to 'reproductive thinking', where thinking about a current problem is influenced by past experience on similar problems even though that experience may be inappropriate. Chapter 4 introduced the 'confirmation bias' in thinking that causes us to seek evidence for a point of view and ignore or fail to look for evidence against it. We can get round working memory limitations by using long-term memory (past experience) and practice (so that actions become automatic). We apply what we have learned, or rely on habits in new situations that are similar to ones we have encountered in the past, because it is usually a sensible thing to do although it sometimes means we might not see an easier way of dealing with a problem. We also get round limitations by relying on in-built biases and heuristics. These are essentially short cuts that allow us to avoid the necessity to deal with all the information available to us by sticking to just the salient bits. This, however, leads to the kind of error that makes us think that £49.99 is significantly cheaper than £50.

This chapter goes back over some of the reasons why we might misrepresent problems and why past experience sometimes does not help in solving new problems. It covers the distinction between surface features of situations and problems and the structural features, and the strong influence of surface thought. It also examines further built-in biases to reasoning that cause us to concentrate on some aspects of a situation and ignore others, and why we appear to be so poor at understanding probabilities. We will begin, however, with the ways that past knowledge can interfere with present behaviour.

Getting set in your ways

Suppose you are given the following task. Before you on a table are three boxes containing tacks, candles and matches as in Figure 5.1. How do you build a platform affixed to a wall that will support a lit candle and prevent wax dripping onto the floor?

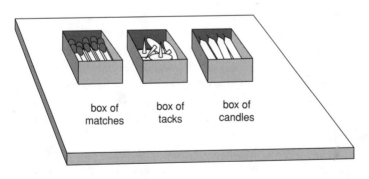

box of
matches

box of
tacks

box of
candles

FIGURE 5.1 Duncker's (1945) candle problem

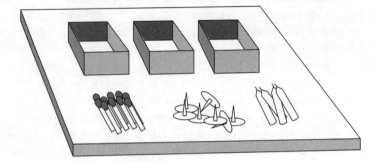

FIGURE 5.2 Version of Duncker's (1945) candle problem where the elements are separated

People given the problem by Duncker (1945), as stated above, were less likely to solve it than if they were given an alternative version shown in Figure 5.2.

The two versions contained exactly the same objects but in the first the boxes were being used as containers. Since the boxes already had a function, people were less likely to notice that they could be used as a platform for the candles. This is an example of a mental set known as **functional fixedness**. Functional fixedness prevents us from seeing an alternative function for an object since their main or obvious function is the salient one.

The same thing was found by Maier (1931) who asked participants to tie two strings together that were dangling from the ceiling. The two strings were positioned such that they were too far away from each other for the participant to reach both with outstretched arms. In the room, however, were a number of objects, including a pair of pliers. The solution was to tie the pliers to the base of one of the strings and swing the string. As the participant held onto the other string he could catch the swinging string and tie the two together. Maier argued that the participants did not notice that the pliers could be used as a pendulum weight since that is not the function of pliers.

Keane (1989) has argued that it is the salience of certain properties of the objects in these problems that is important.

If you see someone using pliers to grip something then the property of gripping tightly would be salient and hence incorporated into your representation of the tool. If, on the other hand, you saw it being used to bang in a small nail you might represent it in terms of its heaviness since that property is salient in this context. In Maier's two-string problem the heaviness may not be seen as salient. In Duncker's candle-holder problem the salience of the boxes as containers is emphasised since they contain tacks, matches, etc. Other possible properties of the box are therefore not immediately represented. The failure to represent completely the properties of objects leads to functional fixedness.

Another type of mental set can be induced through learning a procedure for solving a particular type of problem. This amounts to a habit. When a new situation arises that resembles previous ones where the procedure worked then we are naturally likely to apply that procedure again. Unfortunately, there are cases where that is not the best or simplest thing to do, since a simpler procedure would be even better. The 'habit' prevents the solver from seeing the simpler solution.

In a study by Luchins and Luchins (1959) participants were given a series of problems based on water jars that can contain different amounts of water. Using those jars as measuring jugs they had to end up with a set amount of water. For example, if the jar A can hold 18 litres, jar B can hold 43 litres and jar C can hold 10 litres, how can you end up with 5 litres? The answer is to fill jar B with 43 litres, from it fill jar A and pour out the water from A. you are now left with 25 litres in B, so now you fill C twice emptying C each time thereby getting rid of 20 litres and ending up with 5 litres in jar B.

After a series of such problems, participants begin to realise that pouring water from one jar to another always follows the same pattern. In fact, the pattern or rule for pouring is B – A – 2C (from the contents of jar B take out enough to fill A, and enough to fill C twice (e.g., $43 – 18 – (2 \times 10) = 5$). Having learned that rule people generally failed to notice that the following version of the problem could be solved much more simply:

Jar A	Jar B	Jar C	Goal
23	49	3	20

In fact, it can be solved very easily by pouring the contents of jar A into jar C. Having learned a rule that worked, participants followed it blindly and thus failed to see that a simpler solution could be used.

Breaking free of self-imposed constraints

Breaking free of constraints imposed by either an initial representation of a problem or through a learned procedure (or through received wisdom as in Chapter 3) can be very difficult. For example, we tend to see the nine dots in the problem in Figure 5.3 as a square. In this case, the shape constrains our thinking about the problem and we may not see that the solution involves breaking out of that shape.

Functional fixedness is another unnecessary constraint. We are constrained by the normal function of an object (such as the pliers in Maier's pendulum problem) or by the function we have just seen emphasised (such as the boxes as containers in Duncker's candle-holder problem). A dramatic example of getting over functional fixedness was seen in the rescue of Apollo 13. Ground

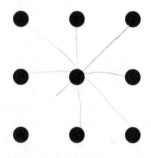

FIGURE 5.3 The nine-dot problem
Draw four lines that pass through all nine dots once only without lifting the pencil from the paper. (Answer on p. 142.)

controllers had to find a way of making a makeshift carbon dioxide filter out of bits and pieces cannibalised from other systems where those bits and pieces had different functions. As mentioned in Chapter 3, breaking free of mental sets imposed by pre-existing habits of thought can be creative. In the film *Speed*, when the villain held the hero's partner hostage the hero broke free of the constraint of not harming his partner and shot him in the leg, thus saving both their lives. Indeed, probably the best Hollywood thrillers concern creative solutions to problems under severe constraints.

Biases in thinking

As the previous sections have shown, we have a bias towards relying on past knowledge of solution methods when we encounter new problems that look the same as ones where the solution methods worked before. Indeed, it would be pretty stupid not to do so. There are, however, a number of other biases in the way we think.

Confirmation bias

One type of bias in human thinking that has been much discussed is the confirmation bias (Evans, 1989b; Evans, Newstead and Byrne, 1993; Evans and Over, 1996; Klayman and Ha, 1987; Wason, 1966). This refers to our tendency to look for evidence to back up our beliefs or hypotheses without necessarily considering the alternatives. The confirmation bias was discussed in the previous chapter as an explanation of why people fail to choose a card in the Wason selection task that would falsify the rule. Various explanations have been put forward for the so-called confirmation bias, including the argument that the term is a misnomer (see p. 92). For the moment we will take a deliberately broad definition of the confirmation bias and concentrate on some examples of the kinds of things that demonstrate it.

Everyday examples of the confirmation bias abound. There are always cases in the news where two sides of a conflict refer to evidence that backs up their belief and ignore contradictory evidence:

- The legal system works by having advocates advocating one side of an argument only.

- In 1998 there were newspaper articles about research that seemed to show that the offspring of women who have stressful or high profile jobs tend to be male. These articles then showed pictures of famous women and their sons. There were no photos of famous women and their daughters; in fact, the possibility was never mentioned.

- You read a horoscope that says that you will meet a tall handsome stranger and later that day on the bus you bump into a tall man who might be considered handsome and so the horoscope is confirmed.

- Advertisers are well aware of this bias and make deliberate use of it. One National Lottery advert read: 'Why wait till the weekend to be a winner?' The advert referred only to the positive aspects (winning) and ignored the negative aspects (the far greater chance of losing) of buying lottery scratchcards.

Scientific method is based on doubt. However, scientists are human beings and subject to the same biases in reasoning as the rest of us, including experimenter bias where they might, often unconsciously, manipulate an experiment to get the results they want. For example, some psychologists believe that nurture plays the dominant role in producing individual differences in intelligence; others believe that nature plays the more important role. Both engage in research activities that back up their beliefs

> Despite ubiquitous claims to scientific objectivity in the production of knowledge, few if any of our efforts at empirical or theoretical science are free of bias. All of our research efforts tend to be influenced by prior knowledge and beliefs concerning the phenomena that we study.
>
> (Gordon and Lemons, 1997, p. 323)

None the less, the point of scientific method is to put one's beliefs to the test by carrying out experiments that other people can replicate. Other knowledge systems rely on belief rather than doubt. Astrologers do not normally try to falsify their hypotheses, although other people have kindly done this for them. They are liable to notice when an event matches a prediction but ignore those events that do not. Occasionally, though, such beliefs do get tested. Touch therapists believe that passing their hands over a patient's body without actually touching it allows them to connect with the patient's 'energy field'. Their belief was tested by an 11-year-old as a science project:

Emily Rosa conducted an experiment to see if the therapists were phonies. Her results were published yesterday by the Journal of the American Medical Association. Her approach was super simple. After recruiting 21 practitioners, she sat them behind a screen and had them put their two hands through holes to the other side. By flipping a coin she decided over which hands she would place one of her own. Not touching but within 'energy field' range. Then she asked the obvious question: over which of your hands is my hand hovering? If the therapists could really detect human energy, which is the claim that underpins their work, they would know. But oops, they did not. In fact they got the answer right only 44% of the time.

(Usborne, 1998)

Another form of confirmation bias is **selective exposure** where 'people maintain their beliefs by exposing themselves to information that they know beforehand is likely to support what they already want to believe. Liberals tend to read liberal newspapers, and conservatives tend to read conservative newspapers' (Baron, 1994, p. 301). People make friends with and join groups and political parties full of people that share the same point of view.

Explanations for the confirmation bias

Here's a little puzzle you can try out on your friends if you really want to annoy them. Wason (1960) gave participants a problem known as the '2–4–6' problem. Participants were told that the experimenter had in mind a rule, and that the sequence of numbers '2, 4, 6' conformed to that rule. Participants were given the task of finding out what the rule was by generating another series of three numbers and asking if that series obeyed the rule. The experimenter answers 'yes' or 'no'. When the participant is sure she knows the rule she is to announce it and again the experimenter answers 'yes' or 'no'. Most participants begin by assuming that the rule is ascending numbers increasing by 2. In fact the rule is any ascending sequence of numbers. Thus the sequence '–37, 408, 309,098' would conform to the rule. People tend to take a long time to get it.

However, it has been argued that this task does not really illustrate confirmation bias – a whole set of possible hypotheses would give '2, 4, 6' and the participant has to guess what's in the experimenter's head. 'Subjects do not know they have been induced to form a hypothesis that is a subset of the experimenter's rule and that all positive tests will therefore confirm' (Evans and Over, 1996, p. 105). If someone entertains the hypothesis 'ascending even numbers', then giving numbers such as 200, 202, 204 might falsify the hypothesis if the experimenter's answer were 'no'. Baron (1994, p. 253) prefers the term **congruence heuristic** which he defines thus: 'To test a hypothesis, think of a result that would be found if the hypothesis were true and then look for that result (and do not worry about other hypotheses that would yield the same result).'

Furthermore if you had wanted to find out if the assertion:

'If it is a raven then it is black'

were true then choosing *not q* (examining all non-black things) would be a complete waste of time since the set of all non-black things is enormous. It's simpler to stick to examining ravens to find out if any are other than black. Klayman and Ha (1987) have argued that the Wason decision task is deliberately misleading: a garden path problem, in fact. They argued that seeking to prove a hypothesis or seeking to falsify it depends on the context. They give the example of a personnel director who doesn't want to hire someone incompetent. The personnel director would be concerned to make sure the candidate fits the bill. They refer to this as a 'positive test strategy'. Its effect is to look like a confirmation bias and is also another example of satisficing. In an alternative scenario someone worried about a single case of a communicable disease going undiagnosed and untreated would be willing to risk mistakenly treating someone who does not have the disease. This is a 'negative test strategy' – examining people who test negative in order to discover any missed cases.

Evans (1989b) argues that there is a 'positivity bias' in reasoning. This is not so much a strategy but a consequence of cognitive failures. The explanation of the confirmation bias is that it assumes that negative examples are equally accessible and yet people choose positive ones. Evans regards this as postulating a 'motivational bias', and argues instead that participants in tasks such as the 2–4–6 task don't try to falsify their hypothesis because they cannot think of ways of falsifying it in the first place. 'Positive information is preconsciously selected as relevant because it is effective to do so given the limitations on human information processing, working memory capacity, and the time available for searching the world for evidence' (Evans and Over, 1996, p. 106). The point is that we have generally effective reasoning strategies that only fail when we are presented with contrived situations where these strategies won't work.

However, in areas other than abstract, logical, garden path problems there is likely to be a motivational need to seek confirmations rather than falsifications. Evans and Over point out that self-confidence and self-esteem can exert more pressure on thinking than any desire to be strictly logical. When something affects our beliefs and attitudes then a confirmation bias makes sense: human beings do not particularly like to be wrong. We want reality to conform to our beliefs, not conflict with them.

We therefore seek out confirmation for our thoughts rather than refutations. When conflict does occur we can either change our beliefs or we can change reality. In other words we try to avoid **cognitive dissonance**.

Cognitive dissonance

According to the theory of cognitive dissonance any inconsistency between cognitions, such as between what one believes and what one actually sees, is uncomfortable and we seek to remove the inconsistency (Festinger, 1957). One of the consequences of the theory is that engaging in a task (doing something boring for little reward) that runs counter to our attitudes (I don't like doing boring things) can cause us to change our attitudes to match our behaviour because of the 'dissonance pressure' created by the inconsistency (maybe the task isn't all that boring really).

In an experiment by Festinger and Carlsmith (1959) two groups of participants were paid money to do a dull and repetitive task and then to tell waiting participants that the task was actually enjoyable and interesting. One group was paid $20 to do the task and the other was paid $1. The group who had been paid $1 came to believe that the task had in fact been enjoyable whereas the $20 dollar group didn't. Cognitive dissonance theory explains this by arguing that the $20 group had a good reason for complying with the experimenter's task (they were paid a lot). The other group were paid very little to do the task and lie to the waiting participant. They experienced cognitive dissonance when trying to match their behaviour (lying) to their beliefs (it was a boring task). They needed some other reason to justify their effort on the task and lying to the participant. One way of removing the dissonance is therefore to believe that the task wasn't so bad after all.

Avoiding the confirmation bias

The confirmation bias can be avoided by reframing the problem such that potential negative aspects become more salient. Klayman and Brown (1993) argued that by manipulating the environment in which a problem is framed you can vary the forms of reasoning people engage in. They got one group of participants to learn about two diseases separately while another group were given information about the two diseases in a 'contrastive' format that highlighted the distinctive features of the diseases. Diagnoses by the latter group were more accurate in terms of the statistical probabilities. Contrasting one theory with another, the good points with the bad points, and so on, is likely to produce a more balanced view of an argument.

Society has instituted procedures to get over the biases people have in their reasoning. In fact, the bias is actively used in the courtroom where lawyers argue for only one side of a case. Peer review of journal articles and the nature of scientific experimentation means that hypotheses get put to the test. Politicians act as if they are never wrong, hence there are several political parties in most democratic countries. The debating style of parliaments means that the institution itself as a system manages to some extent to get round the problems of confirmation bias.

Unlike other biases, the confirmation bias is one that people are sometimes aware of.

Short cuts in thinking

Sometimes the information available to us is incomplete. There can be a degree of uncertainty about the outcome of a course of action or decision. As a result we have developed short cuts to get to an answer which is likely to be correct more often than wrong.

Here are some lottery numbers chosen by three different people:

(a) 21   22   23   24   25   26

(b)   3   8   17   25   31   42

(c)   7   23   40   43   44   49

Who is most likely to win?

Generally speaking people tend to choose sequences of lottery numbers that *look* random (that is, when they don't choose dates of birth or other 'significant' numbers). In the list above, (b) looks more 'random' than the other two sequences. Actually all three have an equal (1 in 14,000,000) chance of winning. Indeed, the chances of the earth being hit by a large meteorite this year are greater than any one specified individual winning the lottery.

The representativeness heuristic

The reason why people choose numbers that 'look' random is because they tend to believe that a sample should have the same properties as the population from which that sample has been taken. For this reason this type of thinking is known as the **representativeness heuristic**. For example, suppose someone notes down a huge number of coin tosses as in (a) in Figure 5.4. Rows (b) and (c) in the figure represent two samples picked at random from the sequence. If the number of coin tosses is sufficiently large an unbiased coin will yield 50% Heads (H) and 50% Tails (T).

However, the proportion of Heads to Tails in a short run may not match the proportion in the long run. This is the **law of large numbers**. People, however, seem to believe in the **law of small numbers** (Tversky and Kahneman, 1971) where a short run is believed to represent a long run (as in (c) in Figure 5.4 which has three Heads and three Tails in a 'random' order). People who make inferences on this basis are using the representativeness heuristic.

Random numbers also generate runs of results that do not superficially appear random as in (d) in Figure 5.4. Not long after the National Lottery started in Britain people used to go to Larkhall in Scotland to buy lottery tickets when it was found that it was the luckiest town in Britain since it produced more winners than anywhere else. However, there is almost *bound* to be a place that produces more winners than anywhere else or a number that comes up in the lottery draw more than any other. In contrast

(a) HTTHTHHHTTTHTTHHHHTHTHTHHTTTTTTHHTTTHHTHTTHTHTHTTT

(b) HTTHT[HHHTTT]HTTHHHHTHTHTHHTTTTTTHHTTTHHTHTTHTHTHTTT

(c) HTTHTHHHTTTHTTHHHHTHTHTHHTTTTTTHHTT[THHTHTT]HTHTHTTT

(d) HTTHTHHHTTTHTTHHHHTHTHTHH[TTTTTTH]HTTTHHTHTTHTHTHTTT

FIGURE 5.4   A large number of coin tosses from which three samples have been chosen

to the representativeness heuristic, people often believe in 'winning streaks' where the outcome seems to break free of randomness. Gilovich, Vallone and Tversky (1985) studied the phenomenon of the 'hot hand' among basketball players: 10% of fans of basketball believed that a player has a 'better chance of making a shot after having just made his last two or three shots than he does after having just missed his last two or three shots' (p. 297). The illusion is similar to the one generated by choosing row (b) or (d) in Figure 5.4. The sequence does not appear random and so the player is seen as being inspired by the muse of basketball.

The most extreme example of the representativeness heuristic occurs where the sample size is reduced to one. This is known as the 'man who' argument (Nisbett and Ross, 1980). In this case arguments based on very large numbers are 'refuted' by appealing to a single anecdotal example. The argument that cigarettes can cause cancer, bronchitis, heart disease is refuted because my grandfather smoked 40 cigarettes a day since he was 8 and died at 80 having being run over by a Porsche as he came home early one morning from an all-night party.

The availability heuristic

Another influence on how we think about situations is how readily we can call to mind evidence that might be relevant. Are there more words in the English language that have the letter R as the first letter or as the third letter? There are, in fact, more words with R as the third letter, but most people say that there are more words with R as the first letter. According to Tversky and

Kahneman (1973) people find it easier to call to mind words beginning with R than with R as the third letter and so the ease with which they recall words biases their judgement.

Here is another example. Estimate very roughly and as quickly as possible the answer to the two problems below:

(a) $8 \times 6 \times 4 \times 2 \times 1$

(b) $1 \times 3 \times 5 \times 7 \times 8$

People tend to estimate the first of the two as larger than the second, even though they contain the same numbers and both multiply out to exactly the same answer. This is because (a) starts with a larger number than (b). The numbers that come first are more salient and hence more 'available' for thought.

This type of thinking can lead to logical inconsistencies. Tversky and Kahneman (1983) asked one group of participants to estimate how many seven letter words there were in a 2,000 word text of the form $- - - - ING$. Another group was asked the same question except that the seven letter word was given in the form $- - - - - N -$. Even though the first form (ending in $- ING$) is a subset of the second form, estimates for the first form were over twice as great as for the second. Again it is easier to think of words that end in ING than that end in $- N -$. When someone gives an estimate for a subset of instances (A in Figure 5.5) that is greater than the estimate given to the set of instances to which the subset belongs (B in Figure 5.5) this is known as the **conjunction fallacy**.

Here is another example:

Linda is 31 years old, single, outspoken and very bright. She majored in philosophy. As a student, she was deeply concerned with issues of discrimination and social justice, and also participated in anti-nuclear demonstrations.

(Tversky and Kahneman, 1983, p. 297)

Participants were asked to rank the following items in terms of their probability:

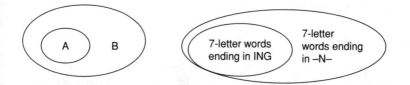

FIGURE 5.5 Estimating A to be larger than B is the conjunction fallacy

- Linda is a teacher in an elementary school.
- Linda works in a bookstore and takes yoga classes.
- Linda is active in the feminist movement.
- Linda is a psychiatric social worker.
- Linda is a member of the League of Women Voters.
- Linda is a bank teller.
- Linda is an insurance salesperson.
- Linda is a bank teller and active in the feminist movement.

In this list 'Linda is active in the feminist movement' was ranked much higher than 'Linda is a bank teller'. However, they rated 'Linda is a bank teller and active in the feminist movement' as higher than 'Linda is a bank teller' despite the fact that the set of people who are both feminists and bank tellers cannot be larger than the set of bank tellers.

The availability heuristic has further influences on our thinking. Air travel is judged much more dangerous after a well-publicised air crash than at other times. Children are driven to school instead of being allowed to walk because of a fear of paedophiles and murderers despite the fact they are five times more likely to get killed by something falling from the sky than murdered. Misjudgements are prevalent when we base our thinking on available information and ignore (or, more accurately, when we don't know) the 'base rate' – the relative frequency of events.

Fallacies in thinking

The base rate fallacy

There are often medical 'scare stories' that influence behaviour. Recently in Britain there was a worry about the Measles–Mumps–Rubella combined vaccine. It was suggested that there might be a link between it and autism. Worried parents prevented their children from having the combined vaccine in favour of the staggered separate vaccines. They did not take account of the fact that the risks of delaying, and of the separate vaccines, were greater than any (as it turned out, vanishingly small if not non-existent) danger from the combined vaccine. Similarly there have been panics over a slight increase in thrombosis caused by high oestrogen contraceptive pills, leading to an estimated 20,000 increase in abortions despite the fact that pregnancy is more likely to be fatal than taking the pill in the first place.

We are often amazed at coincidences and when dreams come true, but our amazement is due to ignoring the base rate. The millions and millions of dreams that people have where something nasty has happened to a relative when in fact nothing has don't get into the newspapers. Out of those millions and millions there will be a few that do come true. Those are the only ones that make the headlines and bolster beliefs in the supernatural. If a coincidence is truly amazing then it must be compared with all the other possible events that occur simultaneously, and there are billions of them. Coincidences *must* be occurring all the time under our very noses, just as long runs of heads in coin tosses must occur. If you deliberately look for them you will probably find them.

Koehler (1996), however, has argued that people do not really ignore base rates, and that findings in the experimental literature are often artefacts of the way information is presented. If people do not know about the frequency of coincidences or the relative dangers of alternative courses of action, then they cannot be accused of ignoring base rates. However, that is precisely the point being made throughout this book. People reflect on the information that is, or is made, salient. That's all they have to go on.

The gambler's fallacy

In Ian Fleming's *Casino Royale*, James Bond has to keep reminding himself, as he plays baccarat, that 'the cards have no memory'. Otherwise he would fall into an entailment of the representativeness heuristic known as the **gambler's fallacy** (or the '**law of averages**'). In row (d) of Figure 5.4 the coin comes down tails six times in a row. If it had come down tails ten times in a row what are the odds of it coming down heads on the next throw? If it had come down tails a hundred times, what would the odds be? In each case the odds are 50:50 for an unbiased coin. It is sometimes tempting to think that the chances of it coming down heads increases with the number of times it comes down tails; but it doesn't. You cannot use past coin tosses, cards, lottery numbers, or any other chance event as evidence for the likelihood of a future outcome in a random process. The roulette player who waits until red appears four times in a row before betting on black, or who doubles the stake on black each time the ball falls on red, is fooling him/herself.

Hill and Williamson (1998) suggest that a person's choice of lottery numbers may be based on the frequency with which the number appeared in the past. In the first 130 draws in the National Lottery 5 had appeared 29 times whereas 37 had appeared only 10 times. Lottery punters may therefore avoid choosing 5 and choose 37 to 'balance' the outcomes.

Wishful thinking

One's desires often tend to distort one's thinking. Most car drivers believe they are better drivers than average (Svenson, 1981). Halpern and Irwin (1973) found that their participants believed an event was more likely to happen if they were going to win money than if they were going to lose money. Weinstein (1980) found that people were unrealistically optimistic about future life events such as living past 80.

Wishful thinking suggests that one might have a degree of control over random events even if that just means that luck is on your side. Thus numbers such as birthdays are used to choose lottery numbers, with the result that few numbers in the high 30s and 40s are chosen. Indeed the organisation of the lottery would presumably be a lot easier if people were given pre-printed numbers; but the organisers know that allowing people to choose their numbers gives them the illusion of control over the outcome. In fact, people may even assume there is some 'skill' involved in choosing lottery numbers. Hill and Williamson (1998, p. 20) argue that 'whereas chance events are seen as passive and wholly uncontrollable, luck encourages the feeling of control through the action taken, with the action having some effect on the outcome'. When gamblers try to choose numbers that no one else is likely to have chosen in order to minimise the number of people they would have to share the jackpot with they are deluding themselves. Thus, a gambler might chose the numbers 1 2 3 4 5 6 since they seem unlikely to turn up. In the 63rd lottery draw when a lot of money was at stake 30,000 other people thought the same way.

Wishful thinking also seems to afflict people who nestle comfortably on the slopes of Mount Vesuvius or build cities along the San Andreas Fault.

Mud sticks: the irrational persistence of belief

A *Monty Python* comedy sketch showed two pilots in an aircraft. One pilot picked up the microphone and said 'Ladies and gentlemen, this is your captain speaking. There is absolutely nothing to worry about.' He then put the microphone down and said to the co-pilot, 'That should get them going.' Richard Nixon, in a famous address to the nation, said, 'There is no white-wash at the White House.' The first case demonstrates that the belief that there is no smoke without fire is hard to shake off. Why did the pilot say that if there wasn't something wrong? Why did Nixon say that if there wasn't something going on? Indeed, in political circles it is well known now that, if there is likely to be any accusation of scandal or impropriety from your political enemies, the best course of action is to get your retaliation in first because the order in which people hear about events is important.

A plausible witness at a trial states that the accused entered a building at 3.30 p.m. Later an equally plausible witness claims the accused was in the pub at 3.30. How does that affect how one thinks of the accused? Unfortunately for the accused, people's thinking can be influenced by the order in which the information is presented. The **primacy effect** occurs when the hearer weighs the first piece of evidence more heavily than later evidence. Asch (1946) gave one group of participants a list of adjectives describing someone as 'intelligent, industrious, impulsive, critical, stubborn, envious' or 'envious, stubborn, critical, impulsive, industrious, intelligent'. Both lists contain the same adjectives but in reverse order. Those participants who heard the list with the positive traits first formed a more positive impression of the man than the group who were given the second list with negative traits first. This is another example of the availability heuristic.

The primacy effect can be understood if we consider the limitations of our information processing system. It is hard to keep all the words in Asch's lists in mind or even to remember them all. The first ones (or the last ones – there is also a matching 'recency effect' at play in certain circumstances) are remembered better and are used immediately as the basis of whatever mental model we build of the person in question. The first couple of words may activate a schema for a particular kind of person and the activated schema is used to interpret the remaining words in the list. So for the first list this will be a fairly positive schema and a relatively negative one for the second list. The availability heuristic means that we process the information that stands out (in this case the information that comes first) and this influences our thinking.

Cognitive dissonance has been used to explain the irrational persistence of belief. Suppose you sell your house and give up your job and give all you have to some charismatic leader who tells you the world will end on 30 December 1999 because he was told so in a telepathic communication with aliens on a planet around the star Sirius. Suppose on 30 December 1999 the world continues to exist. The charismatic leader tells you we've been reprieved and we have another year to live and mend our ways. How do you react? You are more likely to say 'It's a miracle we've been reprieved!' than 'You swindler! I demand my money back!' Going along with the charismatic leader is more consonant with your beliefs than admitting you're a sucker.

If you have a hypothesis 'if *p* then *q*' and you are then told '*not q*', then, as we saw earlier, '*not p*' must follow as surely as $1 + 1 = 2$. If the Turin Shroud was used to cover the body of Christ then the material it was made from must be some 2,000 years old. The evidence suggests that the material is less than 1,000 years old (*not q*) therefore it was not the shroud that covered Christ (*not p*). Despite this the Turin Shroud is probably more revered than it has ever been.

Irrational beliefs can be hard to shift.

The sunk cost fallacy

Another form of persistent irrational belief is the **sunk cost fallacy**. If I made a bad decision that meant that I set fire to £100 and as a result I decided to set fire to another £50 that would be a tad irrational. Yet Nick Leason did this on a much bigger scale when he worked for Barings Bank. This is, however, a type of thinking we fall prey to quite a lot. Suppose you hire a video but you find you don't enjoy it. You might carry on watching anyway because you paid good money for it. Or you might go on holiday when you are still ill and hate every minute of it, but you feel you have to go because the holiday cost a lot of money. This is known in psychology as the 'sunk cost fallacy' (and in biology as the '**Concorde fallacy**'). It afflicts very large organisations as well as individuals. If an organisation has invested a great deal in an enterprise whose outlook is not very rosy, they continue to pour money into the enterprise *because* they have already invested heavily in it. When deciding what to do in the future the past is irrelevant; whatever costs have been sunk into an enterprise are already lost and losing more is not going to bring them back. The Anglo-French Concorde project continued to invest vast sums of money in developing Concorde that they were never likely to recoup, despite huge cost overruns. They continued to do so because it would be a 'waste' otherwise.

Ayton and Arkes (1998) argue that other animals don't exhibit the Concorde fallacy – they know when to quit. Humans often don't, which seems on the face of it to make us more irrational than wasps or blackbirds. So why do we think this way? Ayton and Arkes argue that it is because we are good at abstracting and generalising. Thus we apply general rules such as 'waste not want not' to inappropriate situations. Tetlock (1997, p. 673) argues that we use a strategy of 'defensive bolstering' that causes us to persevere with a failing policy in a vain attempt to recoup sunk costs'. Furthermore, we allow 'labels' to influence us such as the 'status quo' label – the devil you know is better than the devil you don't know.

Most biases and heuristics in thinking are actually useful most of the time. They avoid the cost of relying on our limited capacity to process information and allow us to make fast decisions when necessary. It's not unreasonable to assume that samples of things we encounter are usually representative of the population they come from. Just as visual illusions tell us about how the visual system works by examining how it fails, so thinking is often studied by deliberately trying to find out where it fails. We get a better idea of how thinking works by discovering in what ways it fails to work.

Summary

Gestalt psychologists were interested in how we represent and 'restructure' problems. They viewed thinking as often either reproductive, whereby we use previously learned procedures without taking too much account of the problem structure; or productive, where thinking is based on a deep understanding of a problem's structure and is not structurally blind. Failures in thinking were often due to:

- functional fixedness, when we fail to notice that an object can have more than one use;
- the effects of set, when we apply previously learned procedures when a simpler procedure would work.

There is a range of biases and heuristics that influence our thinking and often affect the decisions we make based on uncertain information. The main belief bias affecting thinking is the confirmation bias where we seek out and notice information consonant with our beliefs. The main heuristic is the availability heuristic whereby we make use of information that stands out and is more immediately 'available'.

We also entertain a number of fallacies such as the gambler's fallacy, where past random events are assumed to influence future ones. The sunk cost fallacy makes us maintain a failed course of action because it would be a 'waste' not to do so. We tend to ignore the base rate when deciding on a course of action, probably because information about base rates is not usually obvious in the real world.

Further reading

Baron, J. (1994) *Thinking and Deciding* (2nd edn), Cambridge: Cambridge University Press. Chapter 4 deals with functional fixedness and set effects. Chapter 15 covers some of the biases and beliefs discussed in the present chapter and adds a few more. The book is recommended as it covers a wide range of influences on thinking.

Evans, J. S. B. T. and Over, D. E. (1996) *Rationality and Reasoning*, Hove, Sussex: Psychology Press. Presents an up-to-date account of the theories of and influences on human reasoning from an academic perspective.

Sutherland, S. (1992) *Irrationality: The Enemy Within*, London: Constable. Discusses human irrationality and is addressed to a lay readership.

Chapter 6

Intelligent thinking

The real problem is not whether machines think but whether men do.

(B. F. Skinner, *Contingencies of Reinforcement*)

What is intelligence?

WE ALL HAVE A GOOD IDEA WHAT intelligence is, or at least we can recognise it when we see examples of it. Unfortunately, defining it is another thing entirely. In 1921 the editors of the *Journal of Educational Psychology* asked 14 famous psychologists to define intelligence and they got back 14 different answers. Two general themes emerged, however: ability to learn, and ability to adapt to the environment. Sternberg and Detterman (1986) repeated the exercise and got 24 different answers that also included the following themes: metacognitive ability (the degree of awareness of one's own thinking), and how a particular culture would define a particular behaviour.

This book will not therefore provide any definition of intelligent thinking since 80% of other psychologists would probably disagree with it. It will look instead at the various aspects of intelligent thinking that have been emphasised by different psychologists in the past and in the present. In doing so the goal is to provide a framework for understanding intelligent behaviour rather than a definition of intelligence. Some views of intelligent thinking make no assumptions about what is doing the thinking. Thus there is no logical reason why entities other than mammalian brains shouldn't think intelligently. How likely is it therefore that we can get machines to think as humans do?

asuring intelligence

One way of examining intelligent behaviour is to give someone a task that requires 'intelligence' to solve it. Some examples are given in Table 6.1.

Intelligence is needed to solve the first example in Table 6.1. If you can't solve it does that mean you are not intelligent? Obviously not: you need intelligence to solve it but you also need the relevant knowledge. If you don't have the knowledge you can't solve it. It would only be a failure of intelligence if you had the knowledge but didn't or couldn't use it for some reason. So does intelligence rely on knowledge?

The second problem in Table 6.1 is different. You don't need knowledge to solve it (except to know what you are supposed to do). There is some relationship between the first two geometric figures at the top that has to be applied to the third to yield one of the options beneath them. You have to transform and mentally rotate elements and this imposes a heavy load on the visuo-spatial part of working memory. So is coping with a heavy load in working memory a sign of intelligence?

The third problem is similar to the previous one in that it involves inducing a relation between the first two terms and seeing if it fits any of the choices. **Proportional analogies** such as these have been long used to measure intelligence. In proportional analogies there is a structure A:B::C:D (A is to B as C is to D) where there is some relationship between A and B that also applies to C and D. The solver's task is to find the C:D pair that shares the same relation. In problem 3, you need to infer a relation that you may never have inferred before. So is intelligence the ability to make inductive inferences?

Some of the early attempts at formalising what intelligence is was carried out by psychologists interested in measuring those aspects of human behaviour that varied from individual to individual. This is known as **psychometrics**. The first modern intelligence test that set out to measure individual differences in intelligence was conducted by Alfred Binet. He and Theodosius Simon had been asked to develop a procedure for distinguishing normal from mentally retarded children in French schools so that

TABLE 6.1 Tasks which require intelligence to solve

---

1   What is wrong with this recursive function?

```
void f( )
{
    int i;
    printf("in f( )\n");
    for(i=0; i<10; i++) f( );
}
```

(from Schildt, 1990, p. 234)

2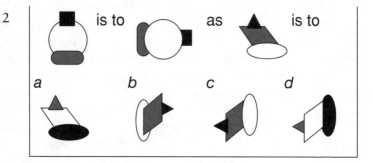

3   anathema : curse ::

      A   charity : saint
      B   pagan : magic
      C   bishop : vestment
      D   prayer : sin
      E   theocracy : state

(see p. 143 for solutions to 2 and 3)

---

the poorest pupils could be given appropriate help. By testing a large enough group of children they were able to determine an individual's 'mental age'. Thus the average 10-year-old child would have a mental age of 10. If an 8-year-old child had a mental age of 10 then the child would have the same thinking level as the average 10-year-old.

This concept was tidied up a little by Stern (1912), who suggested a ratio of mental age to chronological age multiplied by 100. The 10-year-old with a mental age of 10 would therefore have an intelligence quotient (IQ) of 100 ($10 \div 10 \times 100$). The child with a chronological age of 8 and a mental age of 10 would have an IQ of 125 ($10 \div 8 \times 100$).

Eventually, the concept of intelligence started to become bound up with the concept of IQ so that the two became roughly synonymous. The danger of equating the two is that the concept of intelligence becomes circular. It was assumed that we can measure individual differences in intelligence by giving people problems that involve memory, or that test language comprehension, or that require verbal or spatial reasoning. People who are good at doing such tests are so because they have a high degree of intelligence. We know they have a high degree of intelligence because they are good at doing tests of memory, language comprehension, mental rotation, and so on.

The trouble is, measures on a test at any one time do not tell us *why* people differ on these measures. Measuring the speeds of falling objects or the orbits of planets round the sun does not explain gravity. Gravity explains the speeds of falling objects and the orbits of planets round the sun. Similarly we are still left with the need to find an explanation of differences in IQ. In other words we need a theory of intelligence.

Models of intelligence

At the beginning of the twentieth century statistical methods began to be applied to intelligence test items and results in an effort to find out statistically if there were any underlying abilities that

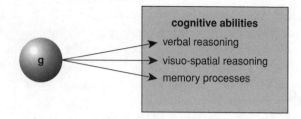

FIGURE 6.1 Spearman's g – a 'mental energy' underpinning specific cognitive abilities

underpinned intelligence. Various researchers proposed various models of intelligence based mainly on statistical techniques that emphasised everything from a single general intellectual ability to a host of specific abilities. More recent researchers have proposed that there are several separate intelligences (Gardner, 1983), or that intelligence cannot be understood outside its cultural context, or that the cognitive processes involved in intelligent behaviour can tell us what intelligence is.

The statistical method called **factor analysis** was pioneered by Charles Spearman. Factor analysis involves trying to find out if responses on IQ tests (for example) cluster together. People who do well on vocabulary tests tend to do well on sentence comprehension as well so there may be some underlying factor (let's call it verbal ability) that underlies both. On the other hand, doing well on verbal tasks may have little to do with how well you do on mathematical tasks so it may be that a different underlying factor gives rise to the performance on mathematical reasoning tasks, and so on. Spearman (1927) argued that there was a main general intelligence factor (g) that underlies the specific factors and that the specific factors were of secondary importance (Figure 6.1).

Thurstone (1938), on the other hand argued that there were seven primary mental abilities (Figure 6.2). There was also evidence of a general intelligence, but the primary mental abilities were more useful to consider. At the furthest extreme, Guilford (1967) proposed a model of intelligence that comprised up to 150 factors (Figure 6.3).

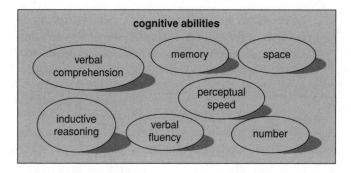

FIGURE 6.2   Thurstone's primary mental abilities

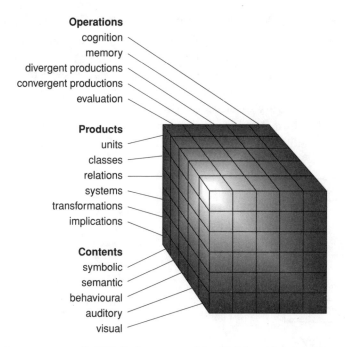

FIGURE 6.3   Guilford's 'structure of intellect' model represented as a cube comprising 150 factors

What emerges from the psychometric approach is a view of intelligence as a hierarchy of mental abilities. Cattell (1971) proposed that the so-called general factor should really be split into two types of ability which he called 'fluid intelligence' and 'crystallised intelligence'. The first of these was a 'content-free' intelligence that is used in coping with novel problems, seeing new relations, and in reasoning inductively. The second kind represents our accumulated knowledge of the world.

Carroll (1993) reanalysed 60 years' worth of data from factor analytic studies of intelligence. This massive undertaking led him to propose a three-layer hierarchy from general in 'Stratum III' to several specific abilities in 'Stratum I' (see Figure 6.4).

Several conclusions emerge from the psychometric approach to understanding intelligence. The first is that the concept of intelligence is in danger of being a circular one, as was pointed out above. This is summed up in Boring's famous phrase 'intelligence is what intelligence tests test' (Boring, 1923, p. 35). The second conclusion is that there seem to be as many models as there are researchers. Psychologists such as Ceci, Sternberg and Gardner, among others, are unhappy with the usefulness, or even the very idea, of regarding intelligence as a unitary power, especially given the wide disparity of views on what constitutes intelligence.

The third conclusion one can come to is that the debate about whether there is a *g* and whether intelligence is mainly due

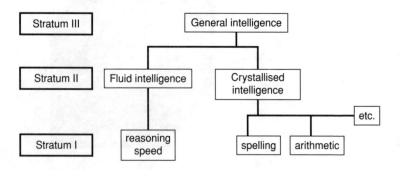

FIGURE 6.4 Carroll's (1993) hierarchical structure of intelligence

to nature (innate potential) or nurture (learned abilities) is very far from over: 'One of the nice things about acrimony in psychology is that if you missed it the first time, you can always watch the reruns' (Hunt, 1997, p. 531).

Information-processing theories of intelligence

When people have a goal and it is not immediately obvious how that goal is to be achieved, they resort to thinking. Thinking involves a set of cognitive processes that attend to relevant information in the environment, interpret that information in the light of prior knowledge, process that information using both general methods such as means-end analysis, analogy and so on, as well as other domain-specific heuristics. If thinking is what you do when you have a goal to achieve, then intelligent thinking reflects how well you do it. Thus there is an interaction between learned and naturally endowed skills and abilities operating on a knowledge base with varying degrees of efficiency such as speed of processing, for example. Indeed, for many years it has been accepted that processing speed correlates with intelligence. Bache (1895) gave American Whites and Blacks reaction time tasks and found that the Blacks' reaction times were faster than those of the Whites. This conflicted with the prior belief at the time that Blacks were intellectually inferior. The contradiction obviously led to cognitive dissonance so, rather that changing their beliefs to fit the evidence, Bache (and others) changed the evidence to fit their beliefs. White people's reactions were slower 'because they belonged to a more deliberative and reflective race' (Bache, 1895, cited in Richardson, 1991, p. 50). Problem solved.

One of the perhaps surprising aspects of the measurement of intelligence is how poorly it predicts how well one does in one's subsequent occupation, despite a high correlation with academic performance such as success in school exams (Ceci, 1996; Sternberg, 1997). A teacher's report on Einstein, for example, said that the boy would not amount to much.

Domain-specific knowledge is not strongly correlated with IQ either. In Table 6.1 most readers are unlikely to know how to start doing question 1. An inability to do this simply means you know nothing about the C programming language. Schneider, Körkel and Weinert (1989) found that children who were highly knowledgeable about football but low on IQ could outperform higher IQ children in tests of reading comprehension, inferencing and memory tasks that involved football. So motivation, prior knowledge and domain-specific cognitive processes can override any differences in measured IQ.

Physical context can make a difference too. Brazilian children who were street vendors can perform complex arithmetic and probability problems in the street which they are at a loss to do once they get into the classroom (Carraher, Carraher and Schliemann, 1985). There have been many studies showing that changing the context of an intellectual task allows children to solve problems they couldn't otherwise solve (such as Piaget's conservation tasks). Ceci and Bronfenbrenner (1985) found that children were better at remembering to do things (prevent cupcakes from burning) at home rather than in the laboratory. Furthermore, the social context (in this case the sex roles) made a difference on how well they performed the task. Older boys in the study did better when the task was couched as a battery charging task than as a cupcake baking task.

So far we have not dealt much with the processes operating on the information coming in from the environment. Sternberg (1977) examined the processes involved in analogical reasoning tasks such as questions 2 or 3 in Table 6.1 and proposed a number of component processes. Suppose I were doing the following problem:

gear : tooth
A   hammer : anvil
B   bolt : nut
C   sprocket : chain
D   girder : rivet
E   screw : thread

The first thing I do is *encode* the word 'gear'. This process presumably involves spreading activation through my mental dictionary so that concepts related to 'gear' are accessed, some of them below the level of consciousness. The next term 'tooth' is encoded in the same way. My next task is to find out what relates 'gear' to 'tooth'. Well, a 'tooth is part of a gear' (the inferred relation here is backwards from the B term to the A term). What happens in the choice items? Well, 'hammer' and 'anvil' are semantically related but an anvil is not 'part of' a hammer, nor is a nut part of a bolt. Is a chain part of a sprocket? No, but a sprocket is part of a chain. Will that do? Not really, because the next component process is *mapping* where the A term has to map on to the C term and the B term should map to the D term, thus:

gear → sprocket
tooth → chain

which doesn't work since they are back to front.

Next item: 'rivet is part of girder'. Maybe. Girders sometimes have rivets. Next item: 'thread is part of screw'? Yes, that seems to fit and they seem to map across. Let's just double check the girder/rivet combination. If we change the relation from 'part of' to 'necessary part of' then the relation applies only to the gear–tooth and to screw–thread. So that's the answer I'll give.

These component processes are given in Figure 6.5.

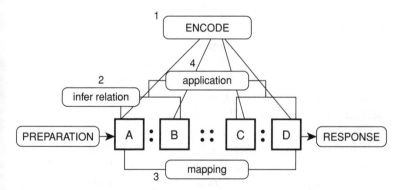

FIGURE 6.5 Sternberg's componential analysis of analogical reasoning problems

Using reaction time experiments Sternberg was able to isolate the times taken to complete each of the component processes in analogical reasoning tasks. One interesting finding was that people who performed best on analogical reasoning tasks spent longest on encoding the terms, and subsequently spent less time on the rest of the task. It seems to be that planning is an extremely important part of successful problem solving. Planning, among other 'metacognitive' skills, is an important part of intelligent thinking. People who spend more time planning an essay in an exam tend to get higher marks because they have worked out the structure and argument in advance, which makes the essay clearer, more concise, and usually more relevant.

Another important influence on intelligent thinking is the way long-term memory is organised. Ceci (1996) argues that the organisation and complexity of associations in long-term memory influence the quality of one's thinking. In trying to understand incoming data the more cues you can pick up the better. If a person's thinking is 'one-dimensional' then they are likely to miss important and subtle distinctions in the world.

Ceci, 1996 (see also Ceci, Rosenblum, de Bruyn and Lee, 1977) proposes a bio-ecological model of intelligence in which intelligence is understood as: (1) a 'multiple resource system' – there are a number of independent factors that go to make it up, including skills, knowledge and domain-general cognitive processes; (2) coming about through an interplay between biological potentials and environmental forces during the course of development; (3) coming about through interactions between the developing child and other people, objects and symbols in the immediate environment; and (4) helped by motivation – exposing a child to a cognitive resource is not enough. The child must be motivated to benefit from the environment just as the Brazilian street children were motivated by the desire to make money (and hence survive).

Robert Sternberg (1985, 1988) has proposed a triarchic theory of intelligence. The theory seeks to explain the relation between intelligence and: (1) its underlying component processes; (2) experience; (3) the external world of the individual. These three aspects 'govern' intelligent action (hence the name 'triarchic').

According to the theory intelligent thinking depends on three main information-processing components:

1   *Metacomponents* are executive processes involved in such things as recognising and categorising a problem, planning, evaluating, and so on.

2   *Performance components* execute the instructions of the metacomponents. The metacomponents generate a plan for solving a problem and performance components carry them out.

3   *Knowledge-acquisition components* underpin learning. They include encoding relevant information and integrating elements into a meaningful whole.

These components interact with experience; hence people deal with unfamiliar tasks differently from the ways they deal with routine familiar tasks that have become automatised.

Sternberg regards context as very important in his theory, but looks at contexts in terms of the individual's goals. We can adapt ourselves to an environment; if that fails we can try to shape the environment to suit ourselves. For example, if you find you can't adapt yourself to the demands or expectations of some of the people you work with then you can try to make them adapt to suit you. If that also fails then change environments (look for a new job). It is primarily here, where intelligence interacts with the external world, that cultural contexts play a part. Adaptive behaviour that is seen as intelligent in one culture may not be seen as intelligent in another. The behaviour of the fairy tale hero who has to perform three arduous tasks to win the hand of the princess may be see as incomprehensibly stupid to a culture that can't see why he can't go off and find another wife.

Another aspect of Sternberg's theory relates to how intelligence is expressed. People have different preferred ways of dealing with problems. Ceci (1996) quotes the mathematician Ian Stewart who tells how Alan Turing once had a problem with his bicycle. The chain kept coming off every so often and he noticed that it would come off at regular intervals. Indeed, he could determine the regularity by counting the revolutions of the front wheel.

Counting the revolutions allowed him to avoid the chain coming off by executing some kind of manoeuvre. Since continually counting the revolutions was somewhat tedious he fitted a counter to the wheel.

> Later he analysed the mathematical relation between the number of spokes in the front wheel, the number of links in the chain, and the number of cogs in the pedal: he discovered that the mishap occurred for a unique configuration of wheel, chain, and pedals. On examining the machine he found that a particular damaged link came into contact with a particular bent spoke. The spoke was duly straightened ... This tale illustrates both the power and perils of logical reasoning. A cycle mechanic would have solved the problem in five minutes.
>
> (Stewart, 1987, p. 386)

Several points can be illustrated by this anecdote. First, people express their intelligence in different ways. Turing may have been a lousy cycle mechanic but he helped decode the German Enigma machine and hence probably ensured the Allies won the Second World War. Second, different types of problems require different types of solutions. Third, Gestalt psychologists would point out the dangerous effects of reproductive thinking: learned patterns of thinking don't always provide optimal ways of solving problems.

Since intelligence can be expressed in a number of ways, Sternberg suggests three main abilities: practical (applying or using what we know to everyday contexts); analytic (using strategies that allow us to manipulate elements or relations among elements in a problem); creative (finding new ways of thinking about problems, e.g., inventing, designing). Figure 6.6 therefore shows a more complex model of the processes and factors that contribute to intelligent thinking. Variation or individual differences in any one of these factors would lead to variations in how well a person performs a task that requires intelligence.

More recently, Sternberg (1998) has referred to intelligence as 'developing expertise'. The measurement of abilities is actually

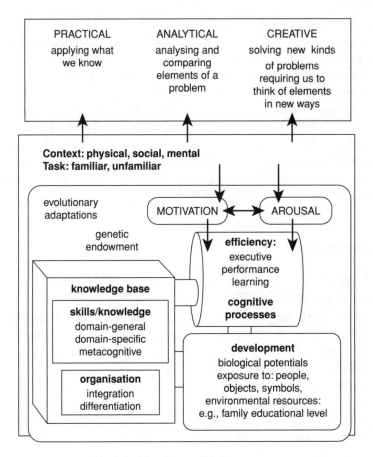

FIGURE 6.6   Model of intelligent thinking

the measurement of achievement – how far one has got along the way to expertise.

Figure 6.6 represents a summary of the various views described so far. Thinking is embedded within a context – physical, social, mental – all of which can influence performance on tasks (familiar or otherwise) requiring intelligent thinking (Ceci and Sternberg are referring to slightly different things when they talk of contexts; see Ceci, 1996). The level of motivation (whether the task is something you are really interested in) will also affect performance; as will the level of arousal – your performance on a task is not going to be all that good if you are half asleep. The knowledge base includes strategies as well as specific knowledge and its organisation is important for picking out important bits of information in any given situation. Furthermore, the course of development from conception influences both the way the brain is 'wired' and the kinds of knowledge we are exposed to (Ceci, 1996). Finally, people have different styles of thinking. They express their intelligence in different ways. However, schools and universities currently emphasise analytical skills over creative and practical ones (Sternberg, 1985).

Machine thinking

Much of the preceding discussion relates intelligent thinking to how a person processes information. However, animal brains are not the only things that process information. Indeed, the whole idea of human thinking as information processing, or computation, comes from an analogy with mechanical systems such as telephone exchanges and, more recently, with computers. If we can pin down the processes people use when they think then is there anything to stop us incorporating those same processes into a machine? The question hinges around whether what brains do and what computers do is fundamentally different.

Artificial Intelligence

Since the invention of computers there have been attempts to build machines that think. The field is known as Artificial Intelligence (AI). As a rule of thumb you might say that a machine is intelligent if it does something that would require intelligence for a human being to do it. This is still rather vague and 'intelligence', as usual, remains undefined. As a partial result of this vagueness AI can mean one of several things. Strong AI is the attempt to *emulate* human thinking. The assumption here is that there is no necessary reason why machines can't have intelligence, which may

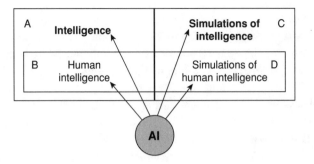

FIGURE 6.7   Where does AI belong?

or may not mean thinking in much the same way that humans think. The left-hand side of Figure 6.7 represents all intelligent things, which includes human intelligence as one example. In 1996 the computer program Deep Blue beat the world chess champion Kasparov. Being able to beat everyone else in the world at chess requires intelligence. The computer that did it made very little attempt to think in the same way as Kasparov, or any other human, thinks. This kind of thinking appears to belong to box A in the figure. It exhibits intelligence, but not as we know it.

Weak AI involves attempting to simulate human thinking by building models that behave in the same way. In this sense a computer model has the same status as a map or an architect's model. The outward appearance is similar to the real thing and the relations between the parts are the same. They are not built in the same way, however, or out of the same materials. Models describe human behaviour and, in so far as they are based on a theory, they also attempt to explain that behaviour. If the computer model runs and does the same sorts of things that humans do, then there is evidence for the theory. Evidence is not proof, however, and the computer model does not think any more than we can live on a map.

A famous early AI program called ELIZA was devised by Weizenbaum (Weizenbaum, 1966) to simulate a non-directive therapist. Non-directive therapists comment on aspects of what the client says without trying to judge or tell him or her what to do. They tend to repeat or throw back what the client has just said so that they can expand on the topic they are discussing. Weizenbaum devised a program that would reply to statements based on pre-programmed bits of sentences and pattern-matching. It might say something like 'Tell me more about . . .' whatever word was used by the client earlier; or if the client wrote 'father' 'sister', then ELIZA might say 'Tell me more about your family.' Words like 'you' would be turned into 'I' and 'I' into 'you' irrespective of what the verb was, which could lead to some bizarre conversations.

ELIZA, however, knew nothing, had no representation of semantics, and had no representation of syntax (grammatical rules for generating sentences) – just pattern-matching rules. It was a simulation of a simulation of human intelligence and so belongs in box C in Figure 6.7.

Another early AI program was Shrdlu by Winograd (1972). It had some knowledge of a limited domain (coloured boxes, blocks and pyramids) and a knowledge of syntax. Unlike ELIZA Shrdlu was an attempt to relate general knowledge to linguistic knowledge so that the computer could understand instructions and 'explain' what it was doing and why. More importantly it is an attempt to model human thinking, so it belongs to box D in the Figure.

One of the difficulties in getting AI to shift from simulations to something resembling 'real' intelligence is trying to get common sense into a machine. Humans are usually unaware of the vast amount of general everyday knowledge that they use to understand simple sentences or everyday events. If you ask a waiter, 'Is there any salt?' he will probably go and fetch you some. A robot waiter might simply say 'Yes' and trundle off. How do you get the human waiter's common sense into the robot? How would it cope with irony: 'Hey, you call this a pizza?'

There are many difficulties facing the robot waiter programmer. How do you get enough knowledge into it so that it can make inferences and conclude that the customer wants some salt? How do you get the system to update its database on the basis of new information and inferences and to keep track of all the possible side effects? How does it know which inferences are relevant and which are irrelevant? How do you get it to stop making inferences? It is possible to infer from your ability to read this sentence that the universe cannot have an infinite number of stars in it, but it's not the kind of inference we are likely to make (the interested reader can look up Ölber's Paradox in an encyclopaedia). These difficulties are known as the **frame problem**.

Dennett (1987) discusses the design of a robot that is designed to remove a spare battery from a room that also happens to contain a time bomb. The first version saw that the battery was on a trolley and that pulling the trolley would bring the battery with it. Unfortunately, the bomb was also on the trolley and this version of the robot failed to conclude that the bomb would come with the battery. The designers set to work on Mark II and made sure it would generate more inferences about the consequences of its actions. Mark II had just finished computing that pulling the wagon out would not change the colour of the walls when the bomb went off. So the designers tried to ensure that Mark III could tell irrelevant inferences from relevant ones, and indeed it sat and whiled away the time categorising all the inferences it made into relevant and irrelevant ones.

There have been many recent AI programs that can write music in the style of specific composers, that can produce novel drawings, that recognise handwriting, that play quite remarkable jazz music, that diagnose illnesses, and we may soon be talking to computers as much as typing into them (as long as they come with subroutines to edit out the curses). Nevertheless, despite the power and sophistication of many of these programs it is still not clear that we are anywhere near moving AI from the right of Figure 6.7 to the left.

Modelling the mind

While there are many AI programs that are designed to do specific things, there are also some systems that are designed to model more domain-general thinking. Such systems are known as **cognitive architectures**. To understand what a cognitive architecture is one can think of the architecture of a house (Anderson, 1993). The occupants of the house need to be protected from the rain, so some form of roof is required. Structures are needed to hold this roof up and walls are needed to keep the occupants warm. Certain parts of the house have to be reserved for certain functions: the occupants need somewhere to prepare food, to sleep, to relax, and so on. There also needs to be some way of getting in and out and windows to let the light in. Like a house, a cognitive architecture contains certain structures that are required to support cognition. Different parts have different functions; some parts might store information, others might process information from the outside, and so on.

There are two main contenders for modelling the architecture of the mind, each of which tends to emphasise different aspects of human cognition. One architecture, known as **production systems**, places the emphasis on the fact that much of our behaviour, particularly problem solving behaviour, is rule-governed and is often sequential in nature – we think of one thing after another. The other contender is **connectionism**. This architecture emphasises the way we can spontaneously generalise from experience of specific examples, and the way we can access a whole memory from any part of it. This architecture is essentially parallel in nature. For example, understanding a sentence such as 'Is there any salt?' requires accessing information about the individual word sounds, meanings, the syntax of the sentence, the intonation of the voice showing it is a question, the context – all at the same time. The waiter understands the question as he hears it; he doesn't stand for several minutes working it out.

Production system architectures

A production is essentially an *if–then* rule. An example would be 'if it rains then take an umbrella.' The 'if' part states a *condition* ('it is raining') under which an *action* – the 'then' part – ('take an umbrella') is triggered. If a set of circumstances matches the condition part of a rule then the action part is said to 'fire'.

A production memory can be likened to our memory for how to do things (**procedural memory**), and can be contrasted with our memory for facts and episodes (**declarative memory**). Declarative memory is memory for facts and episodes such as 'I am having chicken for dinner.' Procedural memory contains memory for doing things such as how to drive a car. A production system architecture has some form of production memory (a *procedural memory*) with other parts bolted on, such as a working memory or a declarative memory, along with connections between them and the outside world. Information from the outside world is stored in a short-term working memory (WM) which can usually hold about five items. These items might match conditions in Production Memory:

CONDITION in WM.	ACTION
If *it is raining*	take an umbrella
	sing
	stay at home
	watch TV

If the condition matches more than one rule then there has to be some way of resolving the conflict (e.g., choose the most recently activated rule; choose the one that best matches the current context).

These architectures model problem solving and the development of expertise. For example, they can model how reading the instructions for operating a VCR eventually turns into knowing how to operate it without referring to the instructions. Examples include ACT-R (Adaptive Control of Thought – Rational) (Anderson, 1993) and SOAR (State Operators and Restrictions) (Laird, Newell and Rosenbloom, 1987). The latter does not include a separate declarative memory. Both models of human cognitive architecture claim to model a wide variety of human thinking. Because of their explanatory power both claim to be *unified theories of cognition* (Newell, 1990).

Connectionist architectures

Computers are pretty poor at doing many of the things that human beings find very easy, such as understanding a spoken sentence or recognising objects such as letters of the alphabet no matter how they are written, or drawing inferences from text. There are therefore important differences between the way human beings think and the way computers 'think'. Whereas the computer metaphor is useful for describing thought processes that operate serially, it does not readily account for our ability to process several sources of information at once. In other words the processing of information that humans engage in is *massively parallel*. If you read the phrase **OASIS AT WEMBLEY ARENA** you would probably understand it immediately. Any kind of 'bottom-up' or serial model of understanding would have to involve a sequence of stages such as: recognising the features that make up the letters (despite the fact that you may never have seen them written in that font), recognising the letters of which the words are composed, recognise the meaning of the words, parsing the phrase, applying general knowledge that Wembley is not a desert and does not harbour an oasis but is in fact a large stadium and Oasis is a popular British rock group. It is more likely that you apply all these sources of knowledge almost simultaneously to arrive at the interpretation of the phrase.

Connectionist architectures (Rumelhart and McClelland, 1986) are particularly suited to pattern recognition and using several sources of information at once. Figure 6.8 gives an example of how activation of words, letters and features together can allow a connectionist system to recognise the word 'TO'. Connectionist systems take their inspiration from the organisation of the brain. Neurones in the brain are connected together in a vast network. Similarly, *'nodes'* in a connectionist network are interconnected. Nodes, just like neurones, will 'fire' if the input to them from other nodes exceeds a particular threshold. Furthermore, the connections themselves have different strengths or *weights*.

If the connectionist network is presented with the word TO then the feature level will pick out the two features that make

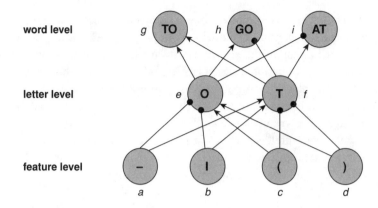

FIGURE 6.8 A connectionist model of word recognition
An arrowhead represents an excitatory connection and a black dot
indicates an inhibitory connection
(Source: McClelland and Rumelhart, 1981)

up the letter T as the first letter and the two features that make
up the O as the second letter. The features that make up the T
have strong links with the letter T at the letter level (and also
presumably with the letters E, F, H, and so on) and inhibitory
links with letters with curved features such as O (and S and C,
etc.). As soon as any activation starts in the system it is propa-
gated through it, so when activation reaches node *f* it fires sending
activation along excitatory links with words that contain T and
inhibitory links to words that do not contain T. At the same time
a similar pattern of activation spreads out from node *e*. Very
quickly the network settles down into a state where the only node
at the word level that will fire is node *g*.

Figure 6.8 is a simplified version of a connectionist system.
Complex systems with several levels can learn to generalise from
the individual examples presented to it. If presented with individual makes of car it will eventually learn to recognise them and
to recognise any new model as a 'car'. Such systems can be trained
to identify abnormal samples from cervical smear tests, for
example, and perform more accurately than humans (they don't
get tired, they don't get bored, and rarely get hangovers).

These cognitive architectures are starting to make the boundaries between cognitive modelling and strong AI rather fuzzy. Anderson has made the strong assertion that 'cognitive skills are realised by production rules' (1993, p. 1). If human beings use production rules and computers can also use them, it may be that there is no essential difference between human and machine thinking. As a result the boundary between human intelligence and machine intelligence is rather fuzzy too. The answer to whether machines could think depends on whether you think there is more to thinking than processing information

Summary

Intelligence is a slippery concept, as few people seem to agree on how it should be defined. Early models of intelligence were based on statistical analyses of scores on IQ tests, making the concept somewhat circular. Spearman postulated a general factor – g – which underlined more specific intellectual abilities. Thurstone argued that there were seven primary abilities, although a small but consistently positive correlation between them suggested that there was an underlying general factor. Guilford proposed as many as 150 factors.

Carroll produced a 'meta-analysis' of studies of intelligence and proposed a three-level hierarchy, putting Spearman's g back at the top with fluid and crystallised intelligence below that and specific abilities below that.

Information-processing theorists are interested in what intelligence is and the processes involved in doing things that require intelligence. Ceci and Sternberg, among many others, regard IQ tests scores as a very limiting and restrictive view of intelligent behaviour. If we can determine the processes involved in human thinking then we can simulate those processes on a machine. Much human thinking – including the errors we make (see e.g., VanLehn, 1990) – is rule-governed and can be modelled by production systems. Much also involves categorising and generalising and can be modelled on connectionist systems. The boundary between human and machine thinking is becoming fuzzier the more we learn about the processes involved in thinking.

Further reading

Cooper, C. (1999) *Intelligence and Abilities*, London: Routledge. Gives up-to-date coverage of the issues involved in IQ and the measurement of abilities.

Sternberg, R. J. (1990) *Metaphors of Mind: Conceptions of the Nature of Intelligence*, Cambridge: Cambridge University Press. This is a very readable account of a wide range of theories that attempt to explain intelligent thinking. Chapter 8 deals with Piaget's theories and his successors, and chapters 6 and 11 cover aspects of Sternberg's own theory (along with others) as well as 'machine intelligence'.

Thinking about thinking

A conclusion is the place where you got tired of thinking.

(Martin H. Fischer)

Beware that you do not lose the substance by grasping at the shadow.

(Aesop, *Fables*)

As we have seen, thinking comes in a variety of flavours. There is mundane, everyday thinking, effortful problem solving, insightful thinking, logical reasoning, and so on. There are also many ways in which our thinking is not entirely optimal. There are biases and even fallacies in the way we think. We tend to use heuristics that don't necessarily lead to correct answers. Despite our experiences, and even because of them, we can get things entirely wrong. Is there anything that helps explain why we think the ways we do?

Here and there throughout the book three influences keep cropping up: salience, similarity and our limited working memory. All of these depend in turn on the trivially obvious point that we have evolved to think the ways we do. People all share the same cognitive architecture – the same organising principles and structures in the mind. Furthermore, human thinking has generally evolved from structures that were already there. Our conceptions (the kinds of things we can think about) are based on our perceptions (Goldstone and Barsalou, 1998). It is no coincidence that 'I see' means 'I understand'. If you throw a ball in the air it continues upward once it leaves your hand, as if the force imparted by your hand is still with it – at least that's what it *looks like*. Our conceptions of force are based on our perceptions of the world.

We have also evolved to take particular notice of anything that stands out from the background and we have survived by making fast decisions based on those salient features. We notice red apples against green foliage, sudden movements out of the corner of the eye, rustlings in the undergrowth, the pattern that faces make. We have learned inductively that the surface features of things are usually very good predictors of their underlying features. This is 'surface thought' and can be very accurate most of the time.

'Fast and frugal' thinking

It is the limitations of our thinking that create the need, at least partly, to rely on surface thought. That way we can usually get answers that are likely to be right even if we don't have all the facts. We can also get the wrong answer even if we have all the facts, because manipulating them puts too much of a load on working memory. It is therefore more useful to rely on 'fast and frugal thinking' (Gigerenzer and Goldstein, 1996). Suppose someone asks you which has the larger population Hamburg or Cologne? Suppose you reply 'I don't know.' Your friend insists, 'Yes, but which do you think is larger?' How do you decide?

Well, you might marshal whatever information you can think of about Hamburg and Cologne. You might recall that Cologne has a cathedral and you get eau de Cologne from there. Hamburg is a port. Is Cologne a port? Hamburg has a premier league football club but Cologne hasn't. That probably means Hamburg is bigger. And you would be right. Are you any more likely to do better if you had a great deal of information at your disposal? According to Gigerenzer and Goldstein more information doesn't necessarily help much and can slow down a decision. They showed that a single good reason is often enough to get a correct answer fast and efficiently. Sperber and Wilson (1986, p. 49) also claim that 'all human beings automatically aim at the most efficient information processing possible. This is so whether they are conscious of it or not.' Why think effortful thoughts when simple ones will give you the right answer most of the time?

The reason this kind of thinking works is because there is often a strong correlation between a salient aspect of a problem (having a premier league football team) and the problem itself (the relative size of a city's population). Thinking can fall to pieces when the salient aspect is not diagnostic of the situation. This gives rise to illusory correlations. This may cause us to believe that nationality predicts meanness, or skin colour predicts IQ. Lateral thinking puzzles rely on our thinking being misdirected by features that appear salient but don't help solve the problem. Even in scientific experiments one can be misdirected. At school we had to light a small candle placed in a dish of water and then had to place a glass over it. After a moment the flame would go out and water would rise up inside the glass. It looks like the flame has burned up all the oxygen, creating a partial vacuum which in turn causes the water to rise up inside the glass. Now, insight problems are often solved by redirecting our attention to some other aspect of the problem that is not at first obvious or salient. To solve the mutilated chequer-board problem you have to notice that the domino has to cover both a white square and a black square. In the case of the candle in the glass, what is not immediately noticeable is that the water rises up *after* the flame has gone out. This little observation means that the burning of oxygen cannot be the main explanation for the effect. When the hot gas inside cools down it contracts, creating the partial vacuum and drawing the water inside.

If you select the wrong features of a problem to build your problem representation around, then the likelihood of solving the problem is reduced:

> If the reasoner fails – for whatever reason – to attend to some logically relevant aspect of the problem then no amount of good subsequent reasoning is likely to lead to a correct solution. Equally, a common cause of bias is that people often attend to – and take account of *irrelevant* features of the problem.
>
> (Evans, 1989b, p. 19)

All of which goes to show that the salient features of the environment are generally good guides to thinking, but they can also at times lead us astray.

Salience can arise from various sources. Some things are salient because we are biologically equipped to pick them out. Some are salient because of our past experience which in turn guides our interpretations of what is going on in the world. The sound a car engine makes may go unnoticed by the driver but may be salient to the car mechanic. Past experience can also lead us to develop naïve views of physical systems. So we don't notice the seven impossible things that happen before breakfast in *Star Trek*.

Past experience is also important in deductive reasoning where people tend to base their judgements of correctness on the content of statements rather than the logical structure. Again, if a conclusion is believable based on our knowledge of the world then chances are it is also logically correct too. We may even be predisposed to reason about some contexts more accurately than others, particularly ones involving 'social exchange' (Cosmides and Tooby, 1992; Ridley, 1997).

Salient aspects of a situation or task in turn can often remind us of our previous similar experience with that situation or task. If you see lots of tables laid out with knives and forks and wax-covered Chianti bottles you may be reminded of restaurants because of the similarity between present experience and past general knowledge. Alternatively you may be reminded of very specific episodes. You see Formica tables laid out with knives and forks and a waiter wearing a red T-shirt and jeans sitting drinking Pastis at a bar and you are reminded of a very similar restaurant that sold wonderful seafood that you ate to the accompaniment of a tremendous electric storm going on outside a restaurant in Avignon. Thus the similarity between present perception and past experience can have a strong effect on thinking through the memory it evokes.

Latching on to the surface features of problems is usually effective. If a problem looks, on the surface, like a problem we have encountered before then we are likely to attempt to solve it using the method we used last time (assuming it worked). This is a sensible thing to do most of the time. The downside is that we don't see a simpler way of doing it. Habit can blind us.

At a deeper level than surface features lie the structural similarities that are found in analogies. The current of water flowing through a channel can help us understand the 'current' of electricity 'flowing' through a wire. Take the analogy too far, however, and you might start worrying about electricity leaking from the wall socket if you leave the switch on and the plug out.

The limits to thinking and their implications

If necessary, we can hold and manipulate several ideas or bits of information in mind at once. However, the finding that we can store around seven bits of information for a short time is, on its own, fairly trivial. The number of items drops if you have to do things with them. You don't really need a psychologist to tell you that either. The important point is the mass of implications that follow. Because we are limited in the information we can process we are swayed by soundbites; we convict someone on the basis of the analogy used by the prosecutor; we rely on stereotypes; we seek confirmation of our beliefs; we reduce complex issues to headlines or simplistic distinctions such as 'left-brain/right-brain' thinking; books whose titles reflect simplistic sex-role differences become bestsellers; we judge books by their cover; we have our palms read or believe our personality has something to do with the position of Venus when we were born; governments decide whether or not to invade a country on the basis of analogies with previous situations (they want to avoid another Vietnam). Simplistic distinctions present us with simple solutions so we don't have to bother thinking through the details. Stereotypes give us a pre-prepared way of judging people and avoid the necessity to judge them individually which is more effortful. We notice the incident that seems to fit in with one of the things it said in our horoscope and don't notice the fact that the other 843 incidents that happened weren't predicted.

Explaining why we use heuristics or why our thinking is biased is not, in general, problematic. We wouldn't have survived if we hadn't learned to make fast decisions under time constraints, or if we couldn't pick out the important features of the environment, or if we couldn't pay attention to one important thing at a time. Unfortunately some of these heuristics and biases are maladaptive in today's society.

Indeed, it is effortful thinking that has to be explained since it is costly in time, effort and energy. A brain gives off a lot of heat, and many women have died giving birth because of its size. Effortful thinking must have given us a competitive edge. Our survival has been aided by our ability to make complex plans and understand the underlying nature of things. This can be characterised as 'deep thought'. It is the degree to which we engage in the latter type of thinking that makes us 'intelligent'. We can plan trips to Mars, build machines that can sit on the head of a pin; we enact laws, write books, analyse arguments; we act in dramas, paint pictures, produce pop records and build tanks; we find ways of conceptualising 11-dimensional space and unseeable quantum events. The list is endless. They are the products of laborious and creative, heuristic and rule-governed, effortful thinking. The question is not whether any one type of thinking is any better than another but when to use them appropriately – and preferably to the benefit of humanity.

Solutions to problems

1   The chain problem (Figure 3.1, p. 47):

The solution involves taking all three links in one of the pieces of chain apart (total: 6 cents) and using the individual links to join up the three remaining pieces (9 cents).

2   The 'geometry' problems (Figure 3.2, p. 49):

The insight involved here is noticing that the two semicircles, shown darker in the figure below, would fit into the white circle. The area to be shaded is therefore equivalent to the square in the middle of the figure. Since the radius is 2 ft the length of the square would be 4 ft so the area is 16 square feet. You don't have enough paint.

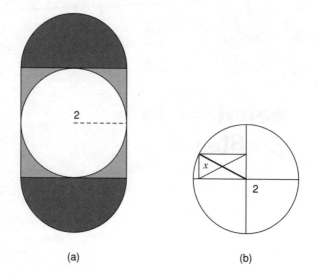

(a) (b)

In (b) the insight is noticing that line x is a diagonal of the rectangle and that the other diagonal which is of equal length is the radius of the circle (2 units). So x = 2.

3   Solution to the nine-dot problem (Figure 5.3, p. 88):

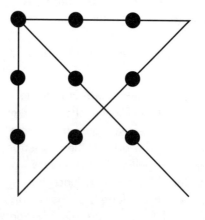

4   Solutions to problems 2 and 3 in Table 6.1, p. 110:

(2)   The answer is *b*. The first figure in the top line is rotated 90° clockwise and the circle has moved to the foreground to cover the square and rectangle shapes to produce the second figure. Rotating the third figure in the top line 90° and bringing the rhombus to the front produces figure *b*.

(3)   The answer is E since the original analogy is an example of category inclusion ('anathema' belongs to the category 'curse' as 'theocracy' belongs to the category 'state').

Glossary

The first occurrence of each of these terms is highlighted in **bold** type in the main text.

accommodation Adapting schemas or creating new ones to deal with new experiences that do not fit into pre-existing schemas.

algorithm Problem solving procedures that are guaranteed to work if specified in enough detail.

analogical problem solving Using a familiar problem to solve an unfamiliar problem. In analogical problem solving the structural features of the analogue (familiar problem) are mapped on to the unfamiliar problem.

analogical transfer Applying knowledge learned in one situation to a new situation.

assimilation Incorporating new experiences into pre-existing schemas.

bounded rationality The degree to which we can attain our goals is limited due to the limitations of our information-processing system and the context in which a task occurs.

cognitive architecture   A theory of the structure of the mind. An architecture describes the functions and modules necessary for the types of thinking and learning behaviour exhibited by humans.

cognitive dissonance   Arises when there is a mismatch or inconsistency in our beliefs or between our beliefs and what we actually see.

Concorde fallacy   *See* **sunk cost fallacy**.

concrete operational stage   Piagetian stage where children develop mental representations they can manipulate allowing them to cope with transformations in conservation tasks, for example. They can see beyond the surface features of situations and problems to their underlying structural features.

confirmation bias   The tendency to interpret information that confirms our beliefs and ignore information that might disconfirm them.

congruence heuristic   Explanation of the confirmation bias that says we look for a result that would be true if our hypothesis were true.

conjunction fallacy   Occurs when someone estimates a subset of instances as greater than the set to which the subset belongs.

connectionism   Cognitive architecture that consists of nodes connected by links that have different connection strengths. Learning or representation consists of adjusting the pattern of weights between nodes.

conservative induction   People tend to be careful about the inductive generalisations they make and therefore they contain a lot of specific detail which may not be relevant.

constraints   Actions that are not allowed or not available.

convergent thinking   Problem solving style where the solver prefers to aim for a generally accepted correct answer.

declarative memory   Memory for facts and episodes.

deductive reasoning   Drawing logically correct conclusions from general statements (premises).

device model   A mental model of a device: how a person thinks a device works.

difference reduction   General term for methods such as means-end analysis or hill climbing that involve assessing the difference between where you are now in a problem and where you want to be, and trying to find a means of reducing that difference.

disequilibrium   'Uncomfortable' state that comes about when aspects of reality don't fit in with a person's knowledge structures (schemas).

divergent thinking   Problem solving style where the solver produces several alternative answers none of which is necessarily 'correct'.

domain   Any area of knowledge from school subjects to air traffic control to house building.

domain-general knowledge   Strategies or other forms of knowledge that can be applied to any domain.

domain-specific knowledge   Knowledge about a specific subject or other topic, including facts and actions appropriate to that subject or topic.

equilibration   Process that removes disequilibrium through accommodation and assimilation.

factor analysis   Statistical technique, involving trying to find out if responses on test items cluster together, allowing the analyst to infer underlying factors that give rise to the clusters.

formal operational stage   Final Piagetian stage where children develop formal or scientific thinking.

frame problem   In AI the frame problem refers to the problem of keeping track of side effects of actions (making relevant inferences) and updating knowledge. The problem is one of how to control the inferences a system can make.

functional fixedness   A kind of mental set whereby a person is prevented from seeing an alternative function for an object because of its pre-existing function.

gambler's fallacy ('law of averages')   The erroneous belief that past outcomes can have some effect on future ones (e.g., that Heads is more likely after a run of nine Tails than after a run of two Tails).

goal state   The end point of a problem – what a problem looks like when it is solved.

H-creativity (historical creativity)   A term used by Margaret Boden to refer to a creative idea or product that no one has ever produced before.

heuristic   Rule of thumb that may provide a short cut to a solution or decision but which is not necessarily guaranteed to work.

hill climbing   A problem solving heuristic whereby a solver takes steps that seem to lead closer to the solution. Used when the goal/sub-goal structure of a problem is not all that clear.

ill-defined problem   A problem where the means of solving it are not immediately apparent.

inductive reasoning   Drawing general conclusions based on specific instances. Induction does not guarantee the truth of a conclusion.

inert knowledge Knowledge learned in one context that is not used in a new context because the person is unaware of its relevance to that new context.

information processing Manipulating (processing) mental representations (information) about the world.

initial state The starting state of a problem (e.g., an essay question and a blank sheet of paper).

law of averages *See* **gambler's fallacy.**

law of large numbers With a sufficiently large number (e.g., of coin tosses) the possible outcomes will be randomly distributed (there will be an equal number of heads and tails).

law of small numbers The erroneous belief that a short run of numbers represents a large number.

liberal induction Sweeping generalisations based on very little evidence – often only one example.

means-end analysis Analysis of the difference between where you are in a problem and where you want to be and choosing a method that will reduce that difference by breaking the problem down into manageable sub-goals.

mental model Generally image-based representation of how something works or how a situation can be imagined.

mental operator *See* **operator.**

mental representation How knowledge about objects, problems, states of affairs, layouts, etc. is stored in the mind. Can be manipulated in ways analogous to the ways states of affairs can be manipulated in the real world.

mental set A form of thinking where one's thinking gets stuck in a rut (without necessarily being aware of it).

modus ponens ('affirming the antecedent') A valid argument of the form 'if p then q; p; $\therefore$ q'.

modus tollens ('denying the consequent') A valid argument of the form 'if p then q; not q; $\therefore$ not p'.

naïve physics Mental models of physical systems such as gravity, friction, evaporation that may not be accurate.

operator An action that can be taken to change the state of a problem (e.g., 'move a ring', multiply, 'take the bus', etc.).

operator restrictions *See* **constraints.**

P-creativity (psychological creativity) A term used by Margaret Boden to refer to creative thoughts or products that are novel as far as the individual is concerned but which someone else may have thought of first.

premises General statements or assertions in an argument (syllogism) from which a conclusion can be drawn.

pre-operational stage Piagetian stage where the young child is beginning to use mental representations to think with. Tends to fail on tasks such as conservation or class inclusion.

primacy effect Occurs when the hearers weigh the first piece of evidence they are given more heavily than later evidence, perhaps because it is better remembered.

primary process thinking Freudian term denoting irrational, instinctual thinking emerging in dreams and symbolic activity.

problem finding Recognising that a problem exists.

problem space A mental representation of a problem that includes all the possible states that can be reached based on information in the problem statement and from long-term memory.

procedural memory Memory for how to do things (often represented as 'if . . . then' rules).

production systems Models of cognition that incorporate 'if . . . then' (condition–action) rules.

productive thinking Generating a possibly novel solution to a problem due to an understanding of the problem's 'deep structure'.

proportional analogies Analogies of the form $A : B :: C : D$ where the relation between A and B is 'proportional' to the relation between C and D.

psychometrics The measurement of human mental abilities.

rationality This can have two meanings: (a) logically correct thinking; (b) thinking that operates to advance our goals. Most often it is the second of these two meanings that is referred to in the text.

representativeness heuristic The erroneous belief that a small sample taken from a very large population should 'represent' that population (e.g., by being equally random).

reproductive thinking Using learned solution procedures to solve a novel problem.

satisficing A combination of 'satisfying' and 'sufficing' whereby someone makes do with the first occurrence, decision, solution, etc. that seems to satisfy some minimal criteria.

schema A mental representation of events, objects, situations, problems. Schemas are structured semantic memory that include 'slots' that contain fixed values (a car schema will have slots for 'engine', 'wheels', etc.); optional values (engine size, colour); and default values that one can assume when specific information is missing (four wheels, petrol engine, etc.).

secondary process thinking Freudian term denoting rational thinking that keeps within the constraints imposed by reality.

selective exposure Ensuring one joins clubs or makes friends with people who share the same values as you.

sensorimotor stage In Piaget's theory this is the earliest stage of infant development. The baby's thinking is influenced by sensations and its limited ability to move around.

source problem Problem, usually in long-term memory, that is being used as an analogy to solve a current problem.

spreading activation Activating a concept (e.g., by hearing it) leads to many related concepts also being activated above some threshold level.

structural features Those features of a problem that are relevant to its solution, and can be used to categorise the problem type.

sunk cost fallacy (Concorde fallacy) Continuing to invest in a loss making enterprise because of the very losses already incurred. The Americans found it hard to pull out of Vietnam because of the lives that were wasted. Some Americans would have preferred to waste more.

surface features Those features of a problem that are irrelevant to the solution.

syllogism An argument containing two general premises (statements) from which a conclusion can be drawn.

target problem Current problem someone is trying to solve using an analogy.

well-defined problem A problem where the solver has available information about the goal state, operators, and constraints.

working memory The dynamic part of the memory system that can store information temporarily (such as memorising a phone number long enough to make a phone call) and that makes decisions about how to process information and access long-term memory.

References

Anderson, J. R. (1993) *Rules of the Mind*, Hillsdale: LEA.

Anderson, J. R. (1995) *Cognitive Psychology and its Implications*, New York: W. H. Freeman.

Asch, S. E. (1946) 'Forming impressions of personality', *Journal of Abnormal and Social Psychology*, 41: 258–290.

Ayton, P. and Arkes, H. (1998) 'Call it quits', *New Scientist,* 158 (2135): 40–43.

Bache, P. M. (1895) 'Reaction time with reference to race', *Psychological Review*, 2: 474–486.

Baddeley, A. D. (1986) *Working Memory*, Oxford: Clarendon Press.

Baddeley, A. D. (1997) *Human Memory: Theory and Practice* (revised edn), Hove, Sussex: Psychology Press.

Baron, J. (1994) *Thinking and Deciding* (2nd edn), Cambridge: Cambridge University Press.

Boden, M. (1992) *The Creative Mind*, London: Sphere Books.

Boden, M. A. (ed.) (1996) *Dimensions of Creativity*, Cambridge, Mass.: MIT Press.

151

Bonatti, L. (1995) 'Why should we abandon the mental logic hypothesis?', in J. Mehler and S. Franck (eds) *Cognition on Cognition*, London: MIT Press.

Boring, E. G. (1923) 'Intelligence as the tests test it', *New Republic*, June: 35–37.

Byrne, R. M. J. and Johnson-Laird, P. N. (1990) *Models and Deductive Reasoning (Vol. 1: Representation, Reasoning, Analogy and Decision Making)*, Chichester: John Wiley.

Caramazza, A., McCloskey, M. and Green, B. (1981) 'Naive beliefs in "sophisticated" subjects: misconceptions about the trajectories of objects', *Cognition*, 9: 117–123.

Carraher, T. N., Carraher, D. and Schliemann, A. D. (1985) 'Mathematics in the streets and in the schools', *British Journal of Developmental Psychology*, 3: 21–29.

Carroll, J. B. (1993) *Human Cognitive Abilities: A Survey of Factor-analytic Studies*, Cambridge: Cambridge University Press.

Cattell, R. B. (1971) *Abilities: Their Structure, Growth, and Action*, Boston: Houghton-Mifflin.

Cattell, R. B. and Drevdahl, J. E. (1955) 'A comparison of the personality profile (16PF) of eminent researchers with that of eminent teachers and administrators, and of the general population', *British Journal of Psychology*, 46: 248–261.

Ceci, S. J. (1996) *On Intelligence: A Bioecological Treatise on Intellectual Development*, London: Harvard University Press.

Ceci, S. J. and Bronfenbrenner, U. (1985) 'Don't forget to take the cupcakes out of the oven: strategic time-monitoring, prospective memory, and context', *Child Development*, 56: 175–190.

Ceci, S. J., Rosenblum, T., de Bruyn, E. and Lee, D. Y. (1997) 'A bio-ecological model of intellectual development: moving beyond h2', in R. J. Sternberg and E. Grigorenko (eds) *Intelligence, Heredity, and Environment*, Cambridge: Cambridge University Press.

Cheng, P. W. and Holyoak, K. J. (1985) 'Pragmatic reasoning schemas', *Cognitive Psychology*, 17, 4: 391–416.

Chi, M. T. H., Feltovich, P. J. and Glaser, R. (1981) 'Categorization and representation of physics problems by experts and novices', *Cognitive Science*, 5: 121–152.

Clement, J. (1983) 'A conceptual model discussed by Galileo and used intuitively by physics students', in D. Gentner and A. L. Stevens (eds) *Mental Models*, Hillsdale: LEA.

Cosmides, L. and Tooby, J. (1992) 'Cognitive adaptations for social exchange', in J. Barkow, L. Cosmides and J. Tooby (eds) *The Adapted Mind: Evolutionary Psychology and the Generation of Culture*, Oxford: Oxford University Press.

Cosmides, L. and Tooby, J. (1995) 'Beyond intuition and instinct blindness: toward an evolutionarily rigorous cognitive science', in J. Mehler and S. Franck (eds) *Cognition on Cognition*, London: MIT Press.

Dennett, D. C. (1987) 'Cognitive wheels: the frame problem of AI', in Z. W. Pylyshyn (ed.) *The Robot's Dilemma: The Frame Problem in Artificial Intelligence*, Norwood: Ablex.

Dennett, D. C. (1996) *Kinds of Minds*, London: Weidenfeld and Nicolson.

Donaldson, M. (1978) *Children's Minds*, Glasgow: Fontana/Open Books.

DuBoulay, B., O'Shea, T. and Monk, J. (1989) 'The black box inside the glass box: presenting computing concepts to novices', in E. Soloway and J. C. Spohrer (eds) *Studying the Novice Programmer*, Hillsdale: LEA.

Duncker, K. (1945) 'On problem solving', *Psychological Monographs*, 58 (whole no. 270).

Evans, J. S. B. T. (1989a) 'Some causes of bias in expert opinion', *The Psychologist*, March: 112–114.

Evans, J. S. B. T. (1989b) *Bias in Human Reasoning: Causes and Consequences*, Hillsdale: LEA.

Evans, J. S. B. T. and Over, D. E. (1996) *Rationality and Reasoning*, Hove, Sussex: Psychology Press.

Evans, J. S. B. T., Newstead, S. E. and Byrne, R. M. (1993) *Human Reasoning: The Psychology of Deduction*, Hove, Sussex: Erlbaum.

Eysenck, H. (1995) *Genius: The Natural History of Creativity*, Cambridge: Cambridge University Press.

Festinger, L. (1957) *A Theory of Cognitive Dissonance*, Stanford: Stanford University Press.

Festinger, L. and Carlsmith, J. M. (1959) 'Cognitive consequences of forced compliance', *Journal of Abnormal and Social Psychology*, 58: 203–210.

Freud, S. (1954) *Interpretation of Dreams* (original German work published 1900), London: Allen and Unwin.

Gardner, H. (1983) *Frames of Mind: The Theory of Multiple Intelligences*, New York: Basic Books.

Gardner, H. (1993) *Creating Minds*, New York: Basic Books.

Garnham, A. and Oakhill, J. (1993) *Thinking and Reasoning*, Oxford: Blackwell.

Gentner, D. and Stevens, A. L. (1983) *Mental Models*, Hillsdale: LEA.

Getzels, J. W. (1975) 'Problem finding and the inventiveness of solutions', *Journal of Creative Behavior*, 9: 12–18.

Gick, M. L. and Holyoak, K. J. (1980) 'Analogical problem solving', *Cognitive Psychology*, 12: 306–356.

Gigerenzer, G. and Goldstein, D. G. (1996) 'Reasoning the fast and frugal way: models of bounded rationality', *Psychological Review*, 103, 4: 650–669.

Gilhooly, K. J. (1996) *Thinking: Directed, Undirected and Creative* (3rd edn), London: Academic Press.

Gilovich, T., Vallone, R. and Tversky, A. (1985) 'The hot hand in basketball: on the misperception of random sequences', *Cognitive Psychology*, 17: 295–314.

Gipson, M. H., Abraham, M. R. and Renner, J. W. (1989) 'Relationships between formal-operational thought and conceptual difficulties in genetics problem solving', *Journal of Research in Science Teaching*, 26, 9: 811–821.

Goldstone, R. L. and Barsalou, L. W. (1998) 'Reuniting perception and conception', *Cognition*, 65: 231–262.

Gordon, E. W. and Lemons, M. P. (1997) 'An interactionist perspective on the genesis of intelligence', in R. J. Sternberg and E. Grigorenko (eds) *Intelligence, Heredity, and Environment*, Cambridge: Cambridge University Press.

Greeno, J. G. (1974) 'Hobbits and Orcs: acquisition of a sequential concept', *Cognitive Psychology*, 6: 270–292.

Gregory, R. L. (1984) *Mind in Science*, London: Penguin.

Guilford, J. P. (1950) 'Creativity', *American Psychologist*, 5: 444–454.

Guilford, J. P. (1967) *The Nature of Human Intelligence*, New York: McGraw-Hill.

Halasz, F. G. and Moran, T. (1983) 'Mental models and problem solving in using a calculator', *Proceedings, Computer–Human Interaction 1983: Human Factors in Computing Systems*, New York: Addison Wesley.

Halpern, D. F. and Irwin, F. W. (1973) 'Selection of hypotheses as affected by their preference values', *Journal of Experimental Psychology*, 101: 105–108.

Hayes, J. R. (1989) *The Complete Problem Solver* (2nd edn), Hillsdale: LEA.

Hiebert, J. (ed.) (1986) *Conceptual and Procedural Knowledge: The Case of Mathematics*, Hillsdale: LEA.

Hill, E. and Williamson, J. (1998) 'Choose six numbers, any numbers', *The Psychologist*, 11, 1: 17–21.

Holyoak, K. J. and Koh, K. (1987) 'Surface and structural similarity in analogical transfer', *Memory and Cognition*, 15, 4: 332–340.

Hunt, E. (1997) 'Nature vs. nurture: the feeling of vujà dé', in R. J. Sternberg and E. Grigorenko (eds) *Intelligence, Heredity, and Environment*, Cambridge: Cambridge University Press.

Johnson-Laird, P. N. (1988) *The Computer and the Mind: An Introduction to Cognitive Science*. London: Fontana Press.

Johnson-Laird, P. N. and Byrne, R. M. J. (1991) *Deduction*, Hillsdale: LEA.

Just, M. A., Carpenter, P. A. and Hemphill, D. D. (1996) 'Constraints on processing capacity: architectural or implementational?', in D. Steier and T. M. Mitchell (eds) *Mind Matters: A Tribute to Allen Newell*, Mahwah: LEA.

Kahney, H. (1993) *Problem Solving: Current Issues* (2nd edn), Milton Keynes: Open University Press.

Kaplan, C. A. and Simon, H. A. (1990) 'In search of insight', *Cognitive Psychology*, 22, 3: 374–419.

Keane, M. T. (1989) 'Modelling "insight" in practical construction problems', *Irish Journal of Psychology*, 11: 202–215.

Kempton, W. (1986) 'Two theories used of home heat control', *Cognitive Science*, 10: 75–91.

Kieras, D. E. and Bovair, S. (1984) 'The role of a mental model in learning to operate a device', *Cognitive Science*, 8: 255–273.

Klayman, J. and Brown, K. (1993) 'Debias the environment instead of the judge: an alternative approach to reducing error in diagnostic (and other) judgment', *Cognition* (Special issue: *Reasoning and decision making*), 49, 1–2: 97–122.

Klayman, J. and Ha, Y.-W. (1987) 'Confirmation, disconfirmation, and information in hypothesis testing', *Psychological Review*, 94: 211–228.

Koehler, J. J. (1996) 'The base rate fallacy reconsidered: descriptive, normative, and methodological challenges', *Behavioral and Brain Sciences*, 19: 1–53.

Koestler, A. (1970) *The Ghost in the Machine*, London: Pan Books.

Kyllonen, P. C. and Christal, R. E. (1990) 'Reasoning ability is (little more than) working-memory capacity?!', *Intelligence*, 14: 389–433.

REFERENCES

Laird, J. E., Newell, A. and Rosenbloom, P. S. (1987) 'SOAR: an architecture for general intelligence', *Artificial Intelligence*, 33: 1–64.

Lamb, D. (1991) *Discovery, Creativity and Problem Solving*, Aldershot: Avebury.

Luchins, A. S. and Luchins, E. H. (1959) *Rigidity of Behaviour*, Eugene: University of Oregon Press.

McClelland, J. L. and Rumelhart, D. E. (1981) 'An interactive activation model of context effects in letter perception: Part I an account of basic findings', *Psychological Review*, 88: 483–524.

McCloskey, M., Caramazza, A. and Green, B. (1980) 'Curvilinear motion in the absence of external forces: naive beliefs about the motion of objects', *Science*, 210: 1139–1141.

Maier, N. R. F. (1931) 'Reasoning in humans II: the solution of a problem and its appearance in consciousness', *Journal of Comparative Psychology*, 12: 181–194.

Medin, D. L. and Ross, B. H. (1989) 'The specific character of abstract thought: categorization, problem solving and induction', in R. J. Sternberg (ed.) *Advances in the Psychology of Human Intelligence* (Vol. 5), Hillsdale: LEA.

Mérö, L. (1990) *Ways of Thinking: The Limits of Rational Thought and Artificial Intelligence*, Singapore: World Scientific.

Miller, G. A. (1956) 'The magical number seven, plus or minus two: some limits on our capacity for processing information', *Psychological Review*, 63: 81–97.

Newell, A. (1990) *Unified Theories of Cognition*, Cambridge, Mass.: Harvard University Press.

Newell, A. and Simon, H. A. (1972) *Human Problem Solving*, Englewood Cliffs: Prentice-Hall.

Nisbett, R. and Ross, L. (1980) *Human Inference: Strategies and Shortcomings of Social Judgment*, Englewood Cliffs: Prentice-Hall.

Ohlsson, S. (1992) 'Information processing explanations of insight and related phenomena', in M. T. Keane and K. J. Gilhooly (eds) *Advances in the Psychology of Thinking*, London: Harvester-Wheatsheaf.

Okuda, S. M., Runco, M. A. and Berger, D. E. (1991) 'Creativity and the finding and solving of real-world problems', *Journal of Psychoeducational Assessment*, 9, 1: 45–53.

Piaget, J. (1970) 'Extracts from Piaget's theory', in P. H. Mussen (ed.) *Manual of Child Psychology*, London: John Wiley.

Piaget, J. and Inhelder, B. (1958) *The Growth of Logical Thinking from Childhood to Adolescence*, New York: Basic Books.

Pinker, S. (1998) *How the Mind Works*, London: Penguin.

Richardson, K. (1991) *Understanding Intelligence*, Milton Keynes: Open University Press.

Ridley, M. (1997) *The Origins of Virtue*, London: Penguin.

Rips, L. J. (1986) *Mental Muddles*, Tucson: University of Arizona Press.

Rips, L. J. (1990) 'Paralogical reasoning: Evans, Johnson-Laird, and Byrne on liar and truth-teller puzzles', *Cognition*, 36, 3: 291–314.

Roe, A. (1952) 'A Psychologist examines sixty-four eminent scientists', *Scientific American*, 187, 5: 21–25.

Rumelhart, D. E. and McClelland, J. L. (1986) *Parallel Distributed Processing: Explorations in the Microstructure of Cognition* (Vols 1 and 2), Cambridge, Mass.: MIT Press/Bradford Books.

Rumelhart, D. E. and Norman, D. A. (1985) 'Representation of knowledge', in A. M. Aitkenhead and J. M. Slack (eds) *Issues in Cognitive Modelling*, London: Erlbaum.

Schildt, H. (1990) *Teach Yourself C*, Berkeley: Osborne McGraw-Hill.

Schneider, W., Körkel, J. and Weinert, F. E. (1989) 'Expert knowledge and general abilities and text processing', in W. Schneider and F. E. Weinert (eds) *Interaction Among Aptitudes, Strategies, and Knowledge in Cognitive Performance*, New York: Springer-Verlag.

Schumacher, R. M. and Gentner, D. (1988) 'Transfer of training as analogical mapping'. (Special issue: *Human–Computer Interaction and Cognitive Engineering*), *IEEE Transactions on Systems, Man, and Cybernetics*, 18, 4: 592–600.

Shiffrin, R. M. and Schneider, W. (1977) 'Controlled and automatic human information processing: II. Perceptual learning, automatic attending, and a general theory', *Psychological Review*, 84: 127–190.

Siegler, R. S. (1998) *Children's Thinking* (3rd edn), Englewood Cliffs: Prentice-Hall.

Silveira, J. (1971) 'Incubation: the effect of interruption timing and length on problem solution and quality of problem processing', Unpublished doctoral dissertation, University of Oregon.

Simon, H. A. (1956) 'Rational choice and the structure of the environment', *Psychological Review*, 63: 129–138.

Simon, H. A. (1966) 'Scientific discovery and the psychology of problem solving', in R. G. Colodny (ed.), *Mind and Cosmos: Essays in Contemporary Science and Philosophy*, Pittsburgh: University of Pittsburgh Press.

Simon, H. A. (1974) 'How big is a chunk?', *Science*, 183: 482–488.

Simon, H. A. (1983) *Reason in Human Affairs*, Stanford: Stanford University Press.

Spearman, C. (1927) *The Abilities of Man*, New York: Macmillan.

Sperber, D. and Wilson, D. (1986) *Relevance*, Oxford: Basil Blackwell.

Stern, W. (1912) *Psychologische Methoden der Intelligenz-Prüfung*, Leipzig: Barth.

Sternberg, R. J. (1977) *Intelligence, Information Processing and Analogical Reasoning: The Component Analysis of Human Abilities*, Hillsdale: LEA.

Sternberg, R. J. (1985) *Beyond IQ: A Triarchic Theory of Human Intelligence*, Cambridge: Cambridge University Press.

Sternberg, R. J. (1988) *The Triarchic Mind: A New Theory of Human Intelligence*, New York: Viking.

Sternberg, R. J. (1990) *Metaphors of Mind: Conceptions of the Nature of Intelligence*, Cambridge: Cambridge University Press.

Sternberg, R. J. (1997) *Thinking Styles*, Cambridge: Cambridge University Press.

Sternberg, R. J. (1998) 'Abilities as developing expertise', Paper presented at the International Conference on the Application of Psychology to the Quality of Learning and Teaching, Hong Kong, 13–18 June.

Sternberg, R. J. and Detterman, D. K. (eds) (1986) *What is Intelligence? Contemporary Viewpoints on its Nature and Definition*, Norwood: Ablex.

Stewart, I. (1987) 'Are mathematicians logical', *Nature*, 325: 386–387.

Super, C. M. (1980) 'Cognitive development: looking across at growing up', in C. Super and M. Harkness (eds) *New Directions for Child Development: Anthropological Perspectives on Child Development*, 8: 59–69.

Svenson, O. (1981) 'Are we all less risky and more skillful than our fellow drivers?', *Acta Psychologica*, 47: 143–148.

Tetlock, P. E. (1997) 'An alternative metaphor in the study of judgment and choice: people as politicians', in W. M. Goldstein and R. M. Hogarth (eds) *Research on Judgment and Decision Making*, Cambridge: Cambridge University Press.

Thomas, J. C. (1974) 'An analysis of behavior in the Hobbits–Orcs program', *Cognitive Psychology*, 6: 257–269.

Thornton, S. (1995) *Children Solving Problems*, London: Harvard University Press.

Thurstone, L. L. (1938) *Primary Mental Abilities*, Chicago: Chicago University Press.

Torrance, E. P. (1966) *Torrance Tests of Creative Thinking*, Princeton: Personnel Press.

Tversky, A. and Kahneman, D. (1971) 'Belief in the law of small numbers', *Psychological Bulletin*, 76: 105–110.

Tversky, A. and Kahneman, D. (1973) 'Availability: a heuristic for judging frequency and probability', *Cognitive Psychology*, 5: 207–232.

Tversky, A. and Kahneman, D. (1983) 'Extensional versus intuitive reasoning. The conjunction fallacy in probability judgment', *Psychological Review*, 90: 293–315.

Usborne, D. (1998) 'Girl, 11, outwits touch therapists', *The Independent*, 2 April.

VanLehn, K. (1990) *Mind Bugs: The Origins of Procedural Misconceptions*, Cambridge, Mass.: MIT Press.

Wallas, G. (1926) *The Art of Thought*, London: Cape.

Wason, P. C. (1960) 'On the failure to eliminate hypotheses in a conceptual task', *Quarterly Journal of Experimental Psychology*, 12: 129–140.

Wason, P. C. (1966) 'Reasoning', in B. M. Foss (ed.) *New Horizons in Psychology* (Vol. 1), Harmondsworth: Penguin.

Watson, J. B. (1958) *Behaviorism*, Chicago: University of Chicago Press.

Weinstein, N. (1980) 'Unrealistic optimism about future life events', *Journal of Personality and Social Psychology*, 39: 806–820.

Weisberg, R. (1986) *Creativity: Genius and Other Myths*, New York: W. H. Freeman.

Weisberg, R. W. (1995) 'Prolegomena to theories of insight in problem solving: a taxonomy of problems', in R. J. Sternberg and J. E. Davidson (eds) *The Nature of Insight*, Cambridge, Mass.: MIT Press.

Weizenbaum, J. (1966) 'ELIZA – a computer program for the study of natural language', *Communications of the Association for Computing Machinery*, 9: 36–45.

Wertheimer, M. (1945) *Productive Thinking*, New York: Harper and Row.

Winograd, T. (1972) *Understanding Natural Language*, New York: Academic Press.

Yaniv, I. and Meyer, D. E. (1987) 'Activation and metacognition of inaccessible information: potential bases for incubation effects in problem solving', *Journal of Experimental Psychology: Learning, Memory, and Cognition*, 13: 187–205.

Index